RAVEN'S
CRY

RAVEN'S CRY

Christie Harris

Illustrations by Bill Reid

Foreword by Robert Davidson and Margaret B. Blackman

Douglas & McIntyre
Vancouver/Toronto

University of Washington Press
Seattle

92 93 94 95 96   5 4 3 2 1

Published in Canada by
Douglas & McIntyre, 1615 Venables Street,
Vancouver, British Columbia V5L 2H1

Canadian Cataloguing in Publication Data
Harris, Christie.
  Raven's cry
  ISBN 1-55054-055-6
  1. Haida Indians—Fiction. 2. Indians of North America—
British Columbia—Queen Charlotte Islands—Fiction.
I. Reid, Bill, 1920-   II. Title.
PS8515.A789R3   1992   C813'.54   C92-091651-1
PR9199.3.H37R3 1992

Published simultaneously in the United States of America by
The University of Washington Press, P.O. Box 50096,
Seattle, Washington 98145-5096

Library of Congress Cataloging-in-Publication Data
Harris, Christie.
  Raven's cry / Christie Harris ; illustrations by Bill Reid ;
foreword by Robert Davidson and Margaret Blackman.
    p. cm.
  Originally published: New York : Atheneum, 1966.
  ISBN 0-295-97221-1
  1. Haida Indians—Fiction. 2. Indians of North America—
British Columbia—Fiction. I. Title.
PR9199.3.H34587R38 1992   92-23934
813'.54—dc20   CIP

Editing by Saeko Usukawa
Design by Barbara Hodgson
Typeset by CompuType Inc., Vancouver, B.C.
Printed and bound in Canada by D. W. Friesen & Sons Ltd.
Printed on acid-free paper

Raven's Cry *is respectfully dedicated to the many gifted native artists who are contributing to the unique color of our west coast while restoring their peoples' faith in a way of life that was remarkably satisfying to a vigorous northern people and also infinitely kinder to the Earth we all share.*

F O R E W O R D

THIS FOREWORD WAS TRANSCRIBED from a taped conversation between Robert Davidson (RD) and Margaret Blackman (MB) on 17 August 1992, specifically on the subject of *Raven's Cry* by Christie Harris. The transcript was edited for publication, and the edited version was amended and approved by both participants.

MB Tell me, when did you first read *Raven's Cry*?

RD I first read it when the book came out in 1966. It filled a gap in my life as a Haida person, in that when I was going to school in Massett, I kept searching through social studies books, trying to find information on Haida people. At one point in my youth, I started to hear the word *Haida* more and more. I didn't realize that I was Haida, and when I started to realize I was Haida, then I wanted to know more about Haida. And so this book helped in starting to fill that gap.

MB I first read it when I was in graduate school, around 1969. I read it because I was studying some historical photographs of Haida villages (including several of Chief 7wii·aa's house) and was looking for more sources of information. What struck me was that so much research had gone into the writing of the story. Even more importantly, behind this story lay the original documents, which I as an anthropologist and ethnohistorian could consult for the information I was interested in. I was struck by all of the research that had gone into the book, and reading it made me hungry for more.

RD I was really impressed with the sincerity and the feeling Christie Harris portrayed. It's a very good attempt at trying to look at history from a native point of view. For myself, being a native, it helped to give me an idea of why we are such a devastated people, spiritually and culturally.

MB I give Christie Harris a lot of credit for trying to portray the history of Haida contact with the outside world through the eyes of the Haida. I can't comment on how successfully she did that, not being a Haida nor living at that particular period of time, but it was a very important step to try to portray history from the native point of view. At the same time, she aimed her book at a general audience, so I think it filled a big need.

RD One of the things that I also found is that *Raven's Cry* was easy to read. The names of people mentioned in it are now becoming more familiar to me, since I've started to dig deeper into history and learn more about the background, philosophy and ideas of Haida culture.

MB For me the book really marked the beginning of a quest. It sent me to the Queen Charlotte Islands to document the historical photographs that I was collecting. It led me to people like Chief William Matthews, who told the side of the story that is alluded to briefly in the book, the account of Chief 7wii·aa, his father and his lineage. *Raven's Cry* launched my career as a student of Haida history, but it can also be read as a children's story. I've read it to my daughter.

RD I see this book as a beginning for a novice who wants to look at the background and history of the Haida. In high school I really wanted to know more about my background. But in our homes, there was nothing mentioned—my parents didn't speak Haida in front of me, though my grandparents spoke Haida—and that was a real setback for me, when I finally realized I was Haida.

In school we talked about Hannibal, we talked about Cleopatra, Alexander the Great, and all the romanticism that went with those people. Later, I was to realize we had our own culture and our own heroes such as Albert Edward Edenshaw, Charles Edenshaw—but there was no information anywhere so that I could relate to them.

MB I think, given the time at which *Raven's Cry* was published, it said something else worth noting. It was particularly important that in the 1960s there was an outsider who was interested in the Haida point of view and in presenting that point of view to a wide readership. It makes a statement when someone from the outside comes in and says, "Hey, this is important history, and this has a right to be heard as well." Granted, Harris took a stab in the dark in trying to articulate Haida emotions and reactions, and how successful she was at that I can't really say. Perhaps some older generation Haida speakers could evaluate that.

RD There are some ideas in the book that I found very angli-
cized, but they didn't bother me. I felt there was a person
making known some of the tragedies that happened to the
Haida people. It gives you an idea about where the alco-
holism, the drug abuse, the child abuse, all those native
difficulties, are coming from.

MB I think, too, that the book was ahead of its time, because
the Haida people in *Raven's Cry* are not the "Other"
encountered by the maritime traders and explorers. Rather,
the Haida people are the central actors in this book; the
story revolves around them. And that makes a real difference. This is the very thing that is being said today, that
we need histories from the perspective of the native people, and that is what Christie Harris attempted more than
twenty-five years ago.

RD For the time period it was good documentation. I was very
impressed, and it really moved me when I read it. And the
illustrations are also, I feel, ahead of their time. When I
first saw the illustrations, I was impressed by the emotions
that Bill Reid put into them. You could feel the smallpox
epidemic. You could feel the storm.

MB To someone who didn't know anything about contemporary
native art, which at that time was really just in its beginning stages, Bill Reid's drawings made clear that there's an
art here that's very much alive. The richness that *Raven's
Cry* pointed to both in terms of historical documentation
and artistic legacy was particularly impressive.

Do you think *Raven's Cry* will stand as an inspiration
for native people to do their own history? I don't know what
effect it has had among native people.

RD People are aware of it. When the book was first published,
it was read. It was a book people knew about. It's certainly
a book I would keep on the shelf as a reference. In this part

x

of my life I'm really going into depth on Haida history and Haida ideas. I'm learning the lineages, the lineage system, the importance of Haida kinship. We have to know our history before we can move on, and this book provides elementary and easy-to-read insights.

MB I do think the book has to be read as one *family's* perspective on Haida history, because it's very much the story of the Edenshaw lineage. Chief 7idansuu's rivals, Chief 7wii·aa and his family, are not portrayed particularly favorably in this book because events are seen through the eyes of the Edenshaw family. So it should not be viewed as a *Haida* history. Probably Haida history was always viewed through the eyes of particular actors and their respective lineages.

RD It's really interesting to work with you, because you have a different approach and you're educated in a different way. Just to be off the subject a little—some of the information that's in your book on my grandmother, *During My Time,* she had said to me or I'd overheard her say to someone, but she'd never explained *why.* Your book makes those things clear.

MB I guess as an anthropologist and as an outsider, I always demanded the *why,* whereas if you're part of the family you don't necessarily demand it. You also made the point several years ago that there's a lot to be learned through doing. I could talk with your grandmother, Florence Davidson, and ask her about a certain mask and a certain dance, but that's very different thing from you, with your dance group, the Rainbow Creek Dancers, getting instruction from her in preparing to perform a dance. Putting on a potlatch and receiving advice and instruction from your grandmother is very different from me asking, "Tell me about potlatches."

RD The experience of having hosted several potlatches has made me realize that the potlatch was always in transition. It was always developing. One of my favorite stories came out of one of the meetings to plan a potlatch that I was hosting. The questions overflowed the answers or the ideas or the information or the knowledge, and so one elder said, "You do it. You know how to do it. You've been doing potlatching for years. We'll follow you." And that gave me a licence to be creative.

My grandmother would explain certain things to me, like a particular song, and I would say to her, "How should I carve the mask?" She'd say, "Make it smile." And then in singing the song over and over and over again, and finally connecting the song with the mask, the song is saying, "7eeyaa aa mee." 7eeyaa means "I'm in awe," and so I said, "Wow, that's why you can make this mask smile, because it's portraying another expression of that idea." And so in learning some of those values and ideas, we're able to add to the development of those songs and dances and also to give meaning to those old songs, those old dances. It was really exciting to discover that.

In doing the songs and dances over and over again, we started to gain confidence. We also felt a little bored, because we'd done them before, so we started challenging ourselves to come up with new ideas, new dances, new masks and so on. And that is no different from how things were back in 1790 or 1450. It's no different because every generation goes through change. Now I feel we have to go through a redefinition of who we are because some of the old ideas don't work. When we start to redefine ourselves, it is no different from a hundred or two hundred years ago when people also went through redefinition.

MB I think that's true with any culture, that there's a constant definition and redefinition of who you are as things change. Culture is always being created. And it's people who create culture. Why can't you create and define traditions for today and tomorrow, drawing upon what you want from the past and what seems meaningful for the present as well?

RD There were three strong forces that helped to change the pattern. First, there were the epidemics that wiped out eighty-eight per cent of the Haida, and then there were the missionaries who instilled their values which are still affecting people today, and then there were the anthropologists. I feel these are the obstacles I had to overcome to become a creative person within Haida culture. I had to confront Christianity. I had to confront the anthropological view of Haida. I had to confront the devastation of the epidemics, because my dad was a product of that. My grandmother was a product of that. Their parents were a product of that. And so those bruises were handed down from generation to generation.

MB We should take up the topic of the anthropological view of things, because that's interesting.

RD When I first came to Vancouver, I met an incredible barrage of anthropologists. I regarded them as people who held the knowledge, and so I was afraid to say anything in front of them for fear of saying the wrong thing. I was intimidated, and it took me years to break through that barrier so I could challenge and also start to be creative within those cultural ideas.

For example, a friend of mine was doing an archaeological dig in Massett, and they found these bone tools. They spent hours and days trying to figure out what these tools were for, what they were. One day we visited a basket weaver, and this basket weaver was still using that same tool. They didn't think to go to the village and say, "Hey, what's this tool?" It's like they held themselves above the native people, like they didn't think we knew anything. I see that happening quite often.

Another example is when I was at the Royal British Columbia Museum. I saw this instrument and I knew what it was for, but I asked, "What is this for?" They said they didn't know. And so I put it together and told them what it was for. I said, "Why don't you people ask us once in a while?"

MB "Cultural representation"—who has the authority to represent a culture—is becoming more and more of an issue in anthropology among native peoples. There is a long history of cultural representation being the domain of academic experts.

RD Well, maybe it's time for us to hold a conference and invite all the anthropologists so they can hear what we have to say. It's time for us to start breaking our own trail.

MB I think it is. Some of the best conferences happen when you bring together anthropologists and native experts to listen to one another and to learn from one another as equals with different realms of knowledge and different ways of approaching things.

RD That's another thing. We have our own scholars, but they don't have a piece of paper to prove that they are scholars. For instance, Uncle Alfred to my mind would have been a scholar, but he didn't have that piece of paper so he wouldn't be invited to a conference.

I feel that the potlatch is the ultimate. It's like your doctoral dissertation, where you are in front of the public, where you are in front of the elders, where you are making statements. And in order to do that, you have to do a lot of research and planning to make sure everything goes right. It is the ultimate test.

MB Learning through potlatching. It's like taking your Ph.D. qualifying exams, I suppose.

RD Absolutely. That's what I was referring to.

MB I think it is exciting now that more and more native people are starting to write their own history. Someday there may be something along the line of what Christie Harris has done, perhaps documenting another family, written by a Haida. I think that would be really good.

RD Yes. A big change has to take place in order for that to happen. You've probably heard the story of the two buckets of crabs: one belonged to a native, one to a white. The crabs from the white man's bucket kept climbing out of the bucket, and finally the native guy said, "How come your crabs are always climbing out of the bucket and mine aren't?" The white man started watching. Every time one of the crabs started climbing out of the native's bucket, all the other crabs started pulling him down. That's a very common and very popular story amongst natives, to warn we don't encourage enough. We have to start acknowledging our accomplishments more. Give more encouragement to those who are doing a great job.

Now that we know about this, what are we going to do about it? That's my question. Where do we start? What can we do about it? We can't just sit around and complain. It's time to start saying, "Hey, let's get started. Let's start repairing ourselves." This can only come from understanding our history. Now that we have access to our own history, we must take responsibility and chart our own direction.

This book gives a little insight into the tragedies that we as a nation went through since the arrival of the white man. Now is the time to overcome those tragedies. The recovery can only come from our efforts.

P R E F A C E

RAVEN'S CRY is the story of three great and greatly gifted Haida Eagle chiefs caught in the tragedy of culture contact along our northwest coast. It is a true story, as a storyteller sees the truth, through the eyes and passions of her characters—a story to whose telling many people contributed. Those contributions I now wish to acknowledge.

When I moved to Prince Rupert, British Columbia, in 1958, I had agreed to write a series of half-hour dramatic CBC Radio scripts on "those great old Indian cultures up there" for broadcast to the schools. Sheer enthusiasm for the research plunged me into years of almost total immersion in native culture out in the field as well as in public and private libraries.

Only one topic defeated me. I could not uncover enough information about one immensely gifted Haida artist, Charles Edenshaw, to fill a half-hour of air time. Government sources produced only a few scant pages in a national museum booklet. Clearly, someone had to provide information about Charles Edenshaw. Someone had to write his biography.

It was after leaving Prince Rupert, after writing several books for young people, that I talked to artist Bill Reid in Vancouver. I discovered that he had wanted to write the book, "But writing is too much work." Also, he was extremely busy with his own jewelry and woodcarving, uncovering the secrets of Haida art for his own work. However, if I wanted to write it, he would willingly serve as my mentor and art consultant—provided I could get some support for the project from the Canada Council.

After initial reluctance to fund a writer who was neither a Haida scholar nor an art connoisseur, the Canada Council approved a modest travel grant for me and an equally modest consultant's fee for Bill. Then, at Bill's invitation, I began to spend hours in his studio, listening to his assessment not only of Haida art but also of the tragedy of culture contact, while he worked away on his own art. My gratitude to Bill Reid knows no bounds. He gave me my first genuine appreciation of what had happened to the aboriginal population along the west coast.

What I needed most of all was input from Charles Edenshaw's family. Bill said little about that, while old friends from the north assured me that the family would never entrust its treasured stories to a white woman. I was actually afraid to tell them I was coming to talk to them. They might say, "Don't bother!"

Yet, when I arrived in Massett—obviously unexpected—I met Charles Edenshaw's daughter Florence Davidson as if by arrangement. And when I introduced myself, she said, "We've been expecting you. We're having a reception for you tonight." The entire extended family turned out to hear what I had to say. And it may have been the objectionable errors in the museum pamphlet I read out to them that led them to agree readily to having Florence tell me about her father.

That summer of '64 is a treasured highlight of my life. Day after day, while our husbands walked the beaches and talked, I listened to that charming, articulate woman tell me the old family stories—generations of family stories.

When I had heard all her stories, though, I knew that this book had to be more than the biography of her father. It had to be the story of three successive chiefs caught in the terrible tragedy of culture contact. I needed to move to Victoria to put all the family stories into historical context, so we took a beach house at Cordova Bay for a year. And there I received invaluable assistance from my friend Wilson Duff, renowned Haida scholar, curator of anthropology at the British Columbia Provincial Museum and later professor of ethnology at the University of British Columbia.

That year, Inez Mitchell, librarian at the Provincial Archives of British Columbia, was unflagging in her zeal for uncovering source material. And my husband, T. A. Harris, skimmed through endless trading ships' logs to provide me with authentic scenes involving the people in my story.

As I wrote each chapter, I sent it off to my editor in New York, and she kept writing back, "Can't you get this Bill Reid to illustrate it?" I kept asking him. He kept saying, "I'm not an illustrator." But, when he came to Victoria to read the completed manuscript, he went through it in silence, laid it down and said: "That's not bad. I'll illustrate it." Then he climbed the fifty-six steps to his car to fetch the beautiful Killer Whale pin he had engraved and presented it to me.

My publisher in New York, Atheneum, had Wilson Duff officially read the manuscript to check its authenticity. The book was published in 1966. For it, I received a medal in Ottawa from the Canadian Library Association for the book of the year for children and a plaque in Seattle for the Pacific Northwest Booksellers' Award. The book went out of print a few years ago.

I am delighted that its new publisher, Douglas & McIntyre, has shown such commitment to both accuracy and artistry. And it is a particular pleasure to me that Florence Davidson's grandson, artist Robert Davidson—who was an interested youth at that long-ago gathering in Massett—has given so generously of his time and his knowledge to write the Foreword and bring this 1992 edition up to date. To him and interested scholars like Margaret Blackman, who also contributed to the Foreword, my gratitude.

Minor changes to the text of the 1966 edition of *Raven's Cry* were necessary for this 1992 edition, to take account of information that has surfaced in the intervening years. New Haida spellings of the names of people and places have also been used, provided by Robert Davidson. A glossary at the back of the book provides a list of these new Haida spellings with their more familiar renderings in historical and ethnographic records.

Christie Harris

RAVEN'S
CRY

Come all ye bold Northwestmen who plough the raging main.
Come listen to my story, while I relate the same.
'Twas of the Lady Washington *decoyed as she lay*
At Queen Charlotte's Island, in North America.

On the sixteenth day of June, boys, in the year '91,
The natives in great numbers on board our ship did come.
Then for to buy our furs of them the captain did begin;
But mark what they attempted before long time had been.

NEW ENGLAND BALLAD

B E F O R E   Y O U
S T A R T   T H E
S T O R Y

"IN THE YEAR '91"—1791—THE SECRET WAS OUT.

It had been out for several years. Captain Cook had stumbled on it. And when his journal was published, the world had gasped.

Russian merchant adventurers had been getting sea otter skins from the native Aleuts in the North Pacific for years. And they had been selling them to the mandarins of China for fabulous prices, keeping the trade a secret.

By mere chance, Captain Cook's seamen had picked up a few pelts along the North Pacific coast of America and had then sold them in China for such staggering sums that they had threatened mutiny when their captain refused to sail back across the Pacific for more furs.

It was almost unbelievable. Chinese merchants would pay hundreds of dollars for one sea otter pelt.

"And you can buy prime pelts for a few glass beads," astounded merchants told their partners. A glitter brightened their eyes. "Why, a man could be wealthy in no time!"

Englishmen and Americans rushed ships into the marine fur trade. And on each voyage they picked up two fortunes instead of one. First, they bought furs for a trifle and sold them for a fortune in China; then they filled their empty holds with Chinese tea and silk and porcelain to sell for another fortune back home.

It was a time for the founding of family affluence. Too many people saw that. Competition grew fierce along the North Pacific coast. Rival traders bribed the native people with liquor. They imprisoned chiefs to force a village to sell its furs. After all, they told their shipmates, these were only savages; they did not really matter; they didn't have fine feelings like civilized human beings.

"Besides," captains said, "we'll never run into this particular bunch of heathens again."

The savages responded with "treachery." Occasionally they became so "bloodthirsty" that they had to be taught a lesson.

Captain Kendrick of the *Lady Washington* taught them one such lesson "on the sixteenth day of June, boys, in the year '91." The old New England ballad tells the story, but only one side of the story.

The other side is just as exciting; and it starts a little earlier. The native story begins at a time when the only sailing ships venturing along the wild northwest coast were those of explorers, like Captain Cook, who were searching for the fabled Northwest Passage to the Orient. And, like the ballad, it begins "at Queen Charlotte's Island, in North America."

So, if you would like to know the other side . . . "Come listen to my story, while I relate the same."

O N E

It was the spring of 1775.

Storms of seagulls eddied and whirled, flashed and dipped and screamed along the west coast of Haida Gwaii, a large group of offshore islands—the Queen Charlottes—lying fifty miles south of the Alaskan fringe.

Haiias and Yatz, tall Haida Indian boys, stood near the northwestern tip of the largest, northern island. A bracing wind lifted their hair. Sunlight brightened the Eagle crests tattooed on their lithe but full-chested bodies. It glinted on their copper armbands as they stood scanning the wild seacoast that stretched away to the southwest.

Haiias had brought the younger boy along the trail from

K'yuusdaa village, where they were visiting. Now he glanced at him in sudden speculation. He parted his lips to speak; but closed them to watch the seagulls, and then the sea.

Offshore, the swells of the Pacific broke on the reefs in a fury at being stopped after thousands of miles of unbroken ocean.

Inshore, a herd of sea otters sunned themselves on the rocks, and frolicked in the surf.

The taller boy, Haiias, watched the embattled reefs. His eyes held a sea rover's joy in the greatness of his sea. Then his gaze ranged farther out. He peered expectantly along the horizon.

Unaware of this suppressed excitement, Yatz watched the sea otters. Never before had he seen so many of them; and never had he seen them so nearly betraying their other, their human, selves. Little family groups caressed one another fondly. Young sea otters romped awkwardly on the rocks, tossing kelp bulbs; and as they moved, their loose glossy coats rippled in the sunlight. Play was more graceful in the sea. And treading water like human beings, mothers threw their pups into the air and then caught them with a glee that set Yatz laughing. "My heart feels good," he said, watching them.

Haiias smiled indulgently at him; Yatz was newly arrived from a small east coast village. He turned to watch the herd, too; but his thoughts were different. His eyes lingered on the dark pelts that were so eagerly sought in the intertribal trading of the northwest coast. All the chiefs in the north wanted lustrous black sea otter cloaks. Tlingits from Alaska would give you copper for the skin; Tsimshian and Nisga'a from the nearby mainland would exchange boxes of eulachon fish grease, and mountain goat horns to steam and carve into spoons. "You see a chief's cloak for yourself?" he teased Yatz.

The other shook his head seriously, and his eyes saddened for a moment. Then he shrugged off his foolishness. Sea otters were glad to give up their fur blankets, he knew, as long as the sea hunters made themselves worthy of such a gift, before and after hunting. "They seem so very human," he murmured to his companion, then immediately flushed. Haiias was training as a sea hunter. "I heard of one carrying her dead pup around for days," he said in lame apology. "They said she wailed and grieved like a human mother."

"Mothers," said Haiias lightly.

"Mothers," echoed Yatz, sighing. He reddened at the other's sharp glance. An heir to a Haida chieftainship did not betray a weak longing for his home. He hid his embarrassment in an affectionate tussle with his dog.

Then he straightened himself with pride. His home was in his uncle's Eagle House at Hiellen near Rose Spit. There was no better place in the world to be. The world had no prouder blood, he had been told, than that of the Eagle chiefs of the Sdast'a·aas Saang gaahl lineage.

People had dubbed their clan "Sdast'a·aas" because its members were as numerous and as ever-increasing as maggots on the carcass of a dead whale washed up on a beach. Yatz smiled now at the amusing flattery of the clan name. Maggots! And Saang gaahl, the name of the noblest family in the big Sdast'a·aas clan, was equally flattering and amusing. People had named the family "Saang gaahl" because, like a *saang ga* diving bird, it made so great a noise with its feasting.

All the Sdast'a·aas were allowed to carve an Eagle at the top of their totem poles; all could paint an Eagle on their possessions. High-ranking members owned additional crests they used to decorate immense cedar houses which, they had long since discovered, were the biggest and handsomest houses in the world. They had many cherished crests to ornament the fifty-, sixty-, and even seventy-foot dugout cedar canoes which, they had also discovered, were the largest and by far the most beautiful canoes in the world. They had many chiefs' names in the

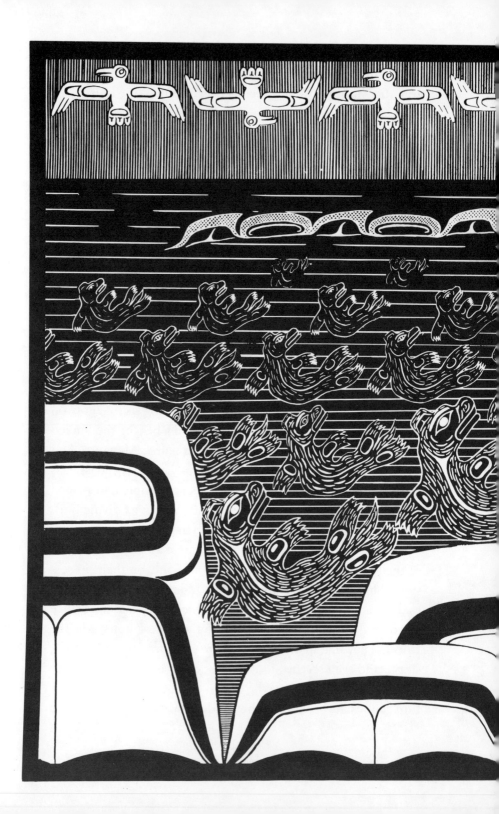

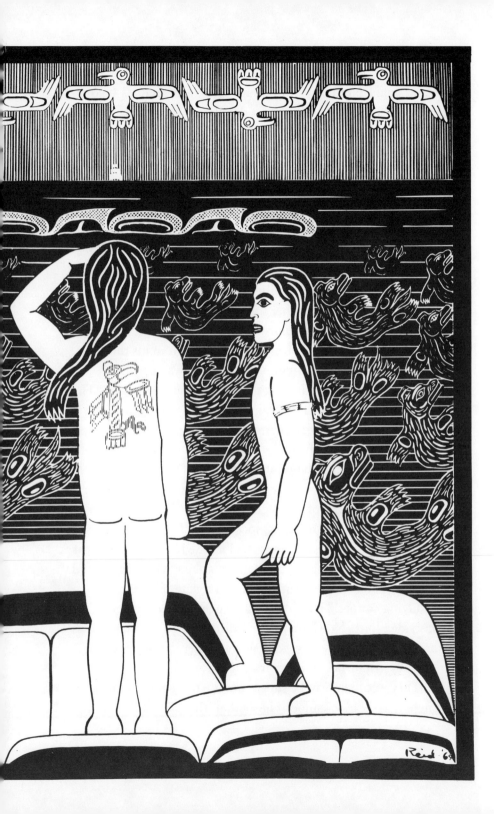

Sdast'a·aas families; and of these none was as honored as the Saang gaahl family's Gannyaa and 7idansuu, names belonging like Haiias and himself at Hiellen, head village of the Sdast'a·aas Eagles.

Still the boy's thoughts kept racing back to the east coast of Haida Gwaii. There, at his father's house, a Raven had topped the totem poles. Raven clans' favorite crest, a Killer Whale, had decorated the high prows of the sleekest canoes his father's skilled hands had fashioned. Yatz sighed, only once more and very softly, for his lost Raven home and for the affection of his father's family. A Haida child belonged to his mother's family, and his mother was a Sdast'a·aas Saang gaahl Eagle. He belonged with her uncle, Head Chief Gannyaa, and with her brother, Chief 7idansuu. Hiellen was his proper home!

Haiias touched Yatz's arm, startling him from his thoughts. "You saw that flash of white?" His voice was eager.

"White?" Yatz peered along the other's pointing finger. "The breakers, you mean? The seagulls?"

Haiias shook his head mysteriously. He parted his lips and seemed to consider speaking.

"What else would be white out there?" Yatz asked him in sudden concern. An uneasy excitement stirred him.

"You have heard of the sightings, Yatz?"

The younger boy nodded, speechless. He scanned the sea with redoubled interest. Rumors had reached his village, rumors that had passed along from village to village with copper and mountain goat horns. But the rumors were too fantastic.

"Flying canoes!" he protested. "Bigger than our canoes!" It was ridiculous. Nowhere in the world were there bigger trees than Haida Gwaii cedars. So how could there be bigger canoes?

"They could be supernatural," Haiias suggested.

"They would have to be supernatural," Yatz agreed with vigor. There could be no canoes bigger than those his father hewed and steamed, each from a single felled cedar tree.

Sea rovers that they were, the Haida knew the whole world of real men and real canoes. They ranged north to the islands of Alaska, and southward for days and days! They knew their ships were unmatched for size and swiftness. This was why they could snatch people from lesser nations along the coast to serve them as slaves.

"With . . . blue men?" Yatz suggested lightly, shrugging off fantastic craft from another world to show Haiias his manly boldness.

But he could not dismiss the notion.

It chipped away at his mind all summer, while his adze chipped away at a Hawk dance mask, and then at a miniature canoe designed to hold whipped berries for the guests at Head Chief Gannyaa's coming potlatch.

Most gifted of the young Sdast'a·aas princes, Yatz worked closely with his uncle Chief 7idansuu, preparing for the winter ceremonies. Sometimes the stone edge of his adze blade broke, and he turned envious eyes on his uncle's carving tool, which was set with a piece of iron. Bits of iron, like rumors, passed along from village to village, and nobody knew where they had started.

Then his dance mask was finished, ready for paint. His canoe was almost carved too. And as he polished it to sleekness with a piece of dried sharkskin, Yatz's eyes caressed its graceful lines and measured its prow for the placing of his Eagle design. He must emphasize the large, curved beak, the Eagle's identifying symbol. And he must fill the space beautifully and precisely with the abstracted elements of the Eagle: wing, eye, tail, feathers. Otherwise, he could do what he liked; and the challenge was exhilarating. He ran his finger along the wood. Smooth as the inner mother-of-pearl of a seashell. He wished he could show his father. Then swiftly he hid his unseemly pride in his own work as two old, old men approached him.

Alert to fine craftsmanship and jealous for Haida reputation, the two old men examined this new boy's work with critical care before they nodded approval. Even a prince, especially a prince, must be worthy of his good fortune in being a Haida.

The village was almost empty; villagers were camped at their ancient family summer stations, harvesting the endless bounty of the sea and the forest and the berry patches. They were gathering and preserving foods with the surging vigor of a healthy, northern people, and with the special enthusiasm of hosts preparing for prolonged feasting.

Head Chief Gannyaa's potlatch was to be the most magnificent gathering the world had ever seen. Along with the conduct of important public affairs, there would be songs, dances, and stories, all brilliantly costumed and lavishly presented. There would be feasting, gourmet feasting; for the Haida had over two hundred ways of preparing just one of their sea foods, salmon. At this potlatch, there would be intriguing new dishes, elegantly served. And there would be gift-giving, hundreds of gifts worthy of the mighty Sdast'a·aas Saang gaahl Eagles. The family must display its glory.

Involved in his own special sphere, Yatz felt his excitement mounting. He almost forgot the flying ship stories in his pride in the preparations.

Yatz and Chief 7idansuu were so busy they could not even go salmon fishing. But they did have to tear themselves away from their paintbrushes long enough to attend a ceremony on the big Alaskan island that lay north of Haida Gwaii, across fifty miles of open ocean.

About twenty-five years earlier, the Haida had driven a Tlingit tribe from the southern part of that island. Still in the process of occupying it, they were building houses on the new sites, and raising totem poles, and inviting relatives from Haida Gwaii to participate in attendant ceremonies.

Yatz and his uncle's family witnessed the raising of a totem pole on the Alaskan island. Then, as quickly as etiquette allowed, they left the new village to hurry homeward.

It was a still, lovely morning; and they were ready to make the dash across the open sea when they saw the swift-moving cloud. "A storm," Chief 7idansuu predicted. "We'll camp here and wait." No Haida ever willingly risked riding out a storm on that treacherous piece of water.

They had not even finished setting up the camp when a small canoe rounded a point and shot towards them. Before it reached them, they had identified it as Haida.

"Chief!" the paddler gasped, leaping out. "A flying canoe!" He pointed northward, beyond the point of land, and his finger trembled. "It is not of this world. We had better hide in the forest."

Chief 7idansuu glanced at his nephew.

Yatz swallowed cold fear, but he nodded in instant understanding. A Sdast'a·aas chief did not hide. His dignity demanded boldness.

Nevertheless, the boy at least felt a drumming in his ears as he and his uncle readied themselves for a voyage to the strange craft. Fringes of dried puffin beaks seemed to clatter like chattering teeth as he lifted regalia from a canoe chest. And he tripped on the fur cloak he carried as he rushed to the chief's sixty-foot state canoe.

Slave paddlers shivered with more obvious panic, but they dared not disobey. The family watched with dismay, yet made not the slightest protesting murmur as a ceremonial plank was laid across the canoe, well back of the bow. In tense silence they saw the Eagle prow slice through the water.

Yatz was also tense and silent.

The canoe rounded the rocky point. Ahead, a sailing ship lay becalmed.

"A flying canoe!"

It stunned them.

"Paddle!" the chief commanded. He himself stepped up onto the ceremonial plank, and his shoulders began to sway under his patterned Chilkat blanket. His head began to move under an Eagle headdress that was hung with many ermine skins and encircled by a tall ring of sea lion bristles.

"A flying canoe!" Yatz only breathed it, again and again, wondering if he were dreaming. His blood chilled in spite of his sea otter cloak, but his steering hand did not falter. His head stayed high under its wooden Eagle.

"Paddle!" he commanded, squeaking the word. "Paddle!" he repeated firmly.

How could this be? There were no trees in the world big enough to make the canoe he saw before his eyes. It might even be a supernatural monster disguised as a canoe for some dreadful purpose. It might even be the spirit of Kali Koustli, from the Land of Pestilence.

"Sing!" he commanded; and once more his voice came out high pitched. "Sing!" he repeated, deeply.

His uncle was already singing. He was shaking his exquisitely carved bird rattle. Now he began to dance on the painted plank. And as he danced, sometimes he dipped his head, wafting a snow of feathers from his headdress, the symbol of peace and friendship.

Yatz steered straight towards the craft. He saw creatures move on it. Monster cormorants? He swallowed panic as he watched the peculiar beings scramble up and down the high, folded wings.

The canoe moved in closer. "They're not cormorants," Yatz whispered in awe. "They have faces like human beings." They had beckoning hands and voices, luring them onto the vessel. To fly them off to supernatural regions?

The youth's mind raced through a thousand stories. Long ago many young Haida princes had been spirited off to incredible adventures. Yet he had never dreamed of it happening now, to someone like himself.

The ship let down a rope ladder.

Yatz blinked his eyes and swallowed.

But his uncle, worthy of the great Haida name he wore, instantly caught the ladder. Less boldly, Yatz moved to follow his uncle. And even less boldly, their attendants backwatered from the awesome ship to wait at a respectful distance.

As Yatz climbed the ladder, his thoughts rushed back to his childhood village. His family would grieve for him, he knew, even as they boasted of his marvelous disappearance. And the Sdast'a·aas Eagles, all of them would watch for his reappearance. Perhaps he would come back with a supernatural wife and children as others had done in the legends! Perhaps he would bring a new crest for the Sdast'a·aas totem poles, a new story for feast-house telling. Yet, gaining the ship's deck, he shrank back from the hand extended to him.

Then he stood with his uncle, dignified, silent, waiting. The canoe would spread its wings and fly off with them. Such things had happened to others in ancient days. Now they two had been chosen for supernatural adventures. His heart pounded within his rib cage.

A breath of wind ruffled the monster wings above his head.

Yatz's darting glances caught small flutters among the feathers. Or were they feathers? Or were they a massed tribe of ghosts in ghost blankets?

Everywhere he saw iron . . . iron . . . iron.

These, then, were Iron Men, come from the source of that mysterious substance. He felt the eyes of the chief of the Iron Men watching his interest in the iron. Then his gaze, like his uncle's, was captured by a shining stick. The stick, only partly wooden, was held by one of the Iron Men.

The observant captain noticed. He spoke to the man. And the man pointed the stick at a seagull.

The Haida watched breathless to see what would happen. Thunder leapt from the stick. Lightning flashed.

"The bird!" gasped Yatz, startled. The seagull had dropped to the sea as though an arrow pierced it. His knees went weak and he sank to the deck. The stick was a supernatural charm; the Thunderbird's power moved through it. He strove to control his unseemly trembling, to remember he was a Haida prince.

Untroubled by a need for dignity, the slave paddlers fled in terror.

A shout from Chief 7idansuu stopped their flight. It also yanked Yatz to his feet again, and straightened his shoulders. A Haida did not show fear, especially a Sdast'a·aas Saang gaahl Eagle prince.

He saw that the paddlers had begun to circle the ship at a safe distance from it. He hoped they would escape, if only to tell the astounding tale at the coming potlatch.

The chief of the Iron Men beckoned Yatz and his uncle to follow him through a door. This astonishing canoe had a house on its back; and inside the house, Iron Men sat around a high plank eating a gruesome meal.

"Maggots!" Yatz shrank in distaste from their steaming rice. "And the grease of dead men!" He concealed his disgust as a seaman poured molasses on his rice. He was thankful they offered him none of the revolting mixture; and he was even more thankful to escape back to the open deck.

All the while his eyes were busy. Truly these were Iron Men. A strange eagerness began to tinge his fear of the coming flight to their supernatural regions. What might he not see!

Still the ghost wings did not spread themselves.

Yatz sensed that his uncle was quite as perplexed. But

7idansuu was a mighty chief in the world of real men. He did not betray his anxieties. Nor did he fail in courtesy. Having noted the pleased surprise with which the chief of the Iron Men had looked at the sea otter cloak, he now lifted it from his nephew's shoulders and presented it to the captain.

The captain accepted it with matching grace. In obvious delight he stroked long black silky hairs that were enriched by a sprinkling of silver filaments. Then he glanced thoughtfully about the ship, and his eyes lighted on the musket. This he presented to Chief 7idansuu, who took it in trembling fingers.

Controlling a natural fear, the chief pointed it at a seagull. But nothing happened.

The Iron chief smiled and took it. He pointed it at a bird and squeezed the trigger. Thunder and lightning leapt out, and the bird fell. Then he handed it back to Chief 7idansuu with foreign words of explanation. And he looked next at the Haida youth, as if wondering what to give him. He spoke to a seaman; the seaman brought something to him; and he presented this gift to Yatz.

What was it? What could it be?

The gift was smooth and shining as a salmon, though shaped more like a yew wedge for splitting cedar. It was hard as a rock. As iron! Yatz held it anxiously by the rounded hole in its thicker end. What was this shining thing?

"Axehead," the captain told him; and he motioned with his hands, like chopping.

A woodworker's charm! Iron shining with supernatural power! He dared to touch its cutting edge. It was sharper than a broken shell. Harder than a pointed elk horn. But—perhaps it would not work for him, as the thunderstick had not worked for his uncle.

The ghost blankets began to stir in the huge white wings above his head.

Yatz gasped. He held his breath. Now they would fly off to the land of the Iron Men.

The Iron chief shouted orders. He indicated his guests' departure.

They both blinked with surprise.

They were not to be carried off?

Without betraying his vast relief, Chief 7idansuu called his paddlers, who apprehensively moved in to get him. Yatz controlled himself, not to depart in unbefitting panic. But he sank down most thankfully into the real Haida canoe paddled by real human beings.

With the rest of the marveling men, he watched the amazing canoe move off. It moved without paddles as the Iron Men sang a strange song. But it did not spread its wings and take to the air, though they watched it to the far horizon. Perhaps, they decided, it waited until no human eye could see it.

And then, spurred by a wild wish to tell someone about this wonder, the crew almost lifted the canoe from the sea with mighty strokes of their paddles. They shouted and sang to give vent to their excitement. They became almost incoherent, blurting out the tale to the waiting family. They couldn't wait to get back home to astound all the villagers.

Impatiently they sat out the storm, then dashed madly across the ocean. But to their disappointment, the villagers were still away at their fishing stations.

Yatz woke every morning before the raven's cry roused Hiellen. If only Haiias would hurry home!

While he waited, he helped his uncle plan a new glory for the coming potlatch. Now they would present a new tale, "The Tale of the Flying Canoe." They planned the production in a ferment of excitement. Yet no matter how they tried, they could not make the thunderstick thunder. Chief 7idansuu pointed it at a thousand seagulls. He squeezed and resqueezed the trigger. But the thunderstick just kept silent. "I have not the *power* to use it," he confessed sorrowfully to Yatz.

The axehead was a different matter! Yatz gazed at it again and again in wonder. He marveled, for he had the power to use the axehead. He chipped with it reverently, and rejoiced at the skill it gave him. Even when he hung it around his neck—it had a hole for a leather thong—the power flowed through his body and into his busy fingers. He carved with a new excitement.

His uncle's eyes shone with pride at the things his pupil fashioned. Then they strayed to the wondrous axehead, and the wood sculptor's eyes grew wistful.

Day after day after day, the raven's cry woke the village, and it was still an almost empty village.

Then at last the villagers returned. People listened, open mouthed, to the tale of the incredible encounter. They babbled exuberantly.

"*You* saw the flying canoe!" Haiias accused Yatz. "*You* saw the Iron Men!" He fumed with frustration and loped along the trail to the open sea again and again to scan the far horizon.

Meanwhile, winter crept towards the village. Visitors arrived for Chief Gannyaa's potlatch, Yatz's own family among them. Flames leapt in gigantic cedar houses. Hiellen swirled with color, with the fantastic dances of a vigorous and artistic people who had plenty of food and leisure and a compulsion to excel. Youths whipped up soapberries into a bittersweet pink froth that was piled into miniature canoes for serving; and guests sucked in the rosy dessert from tiny decorated paddles.

The potlatch was indeed the most magnificent gathering the world had ever seen. They all agreed. The enacted "Tale of the Flying Canoe" was the wonder of it. The thunderstick and the axehead were the glory of the gathering, and Yatz was highly honored. He, the people realized, he, a prince of the Sdast'a·aas

Saang gaahl Eagles and a future Chief 7idansuu, had been supernaturally chosen to become the world's greatest carver.

"My heart feels good," he confided to his young sister Maada.

"My heart sings for you," she told him, and followed him with adoring eyes.

The only one who viewed the axehead with some alarm was Yatz's mother. She drew him aside one morning. "That flying canoe could have been the spirit of Kali Koustli," she said, shuddering at what might have been. She laid a fond hand on her son's arm, betraying how much she had missed him.

"Pfft!" he scoffed, as carelessly as though the dreadful thought of pestilence had never entered his mind . . . and as though he had never missed her. "Have no concern for me! Only good spirits have come to me with the axehead . . . and a little proper respect," he added, grinning at Maada and Haiias.

Those two hung on his every word, now. They asked him a million questions. They looked wistfully at the far horizon, then enviously at Yatz.

"Will the Iron Men come again?" they kept imploring him.

T W O

MAADA'S WEDDING CLOAK was of sea otter pelts, fur side inside. Its outer surface was tinted a lovely marine blue; and as Yatz put the last fine line of black paint on its stylized Eagle decoration, his eyes glowed with an artist's satisfaction and with a young man's pride in his skill. "My heart feels good," he said, gazing at it.

"She will look beautiful," Haiias said almost reverently; for Yatz's little sister had grown into a tall, handsome lady. She was now almost seventeen.

Yatz nodded. But even as he nodded, the glow faded from his features. "I wish Chief Koyah were younger for her," he said, jabbing the air with his painting stick. "I wish that other one..."

That other one, the first choice of the Sdast'a·aas Eagles for their highest-ranking princess, had been killed on a raid. He had been young and full of laughter.

"Koyah is too ambitious," Yatz went on, explosively.

"If a chief can be too ambitious," Haiias agreed, temporizing. All Haida were so rich and energetic, his shrug seemed to say, that it took monumental effort for a chief to raise his standing among the chiefs.

Yatz's eyes flashed. "Ambition can become greed," he snapped. He glared angrily at the wedding cloak. But gradually his features relaxed again into pleasurable excitement. How Maada would sparkle in it!

The two young men had planned the cloak together; for, since Maada was a Sdast'a·aas Eagle princess, Haiias regarded her as his sister also. He had hunted the sea otter in the cold moons, when fur was most deep and glossy. He had watched women cure the skins and sew them into a luxurious garment. Yatz had prepared the blue-green paint for the outer surface. He had traded carved horn spoons for rare, blue-green abalone mother-of-pearl for border ornamentation: Haida abalone shells were lined with a paler, more silvery-rose iridescence. He had ordered the precise placing of the shining discs. Then he had designed and painted an Eagle across the back of the robe.

To match the wedding cloak, a chieftainess had woven a spruce-root canoe hat, raising its crown high with rings of rank. And when it, too, was tinted blue-green in the tradition of Sdast'a·aas girls, Yatz had painted the proud crest on it as well, designing it in the Haida fashion, with the Eagle split into two encircling profiles joined at beak and tail. Human eyes for the mythological bird were of blue-green abalone.

"I wish Koyah were younger for her," he said once again. Maada was a fond and spirited sister; she was very dear to her brother.

He wished it even more sorrowfully later, as he watched her leave her own family and friends in a gigantic canoe paddled by her slaves and Koyah's. The chief's two older wives stood with her, both jealously eyeing Maada. Their black fur robes were brightened by many copper anklets and bracelets and by clusters of copper earrings. Near the group was Chisalgas, Koyah's heir, a handsome young chieftain in Raven regalia.

Yatz's eyes lingered on the heir. If Maada could have married him! "Koyah is too old for her, and too ambitious," he muttered to himself under the farewell chanting. "He is even too small for her."

Koyah was small but mighty. Head chief of a famous clan in the gale-swept southern tip of the Haida islands, he sent his sea hunters out into wealthy waters. He sent his warriors up and down the mainland coast on slave raids. He presented slaves, the supreme gift, at his potlatches. He traded slaves to Alaskan chiefs for native copper so that small copper shields glinted in the firelight of his feasthouse, proclaiming his wealth. And now, to crown his surging prestige, he had managed to marry Maada. He seemed to gloat, smug in his sea otter skins behind the high, fierce prow of his Killer Whale canoe.

The young man's mouth set grimly, watching them go. There would be no young joy between them as there was between Yatz himself and his wife, an Alaskan Raven princess. The older wives would always be hovering, jealous. Poor, slender, stately Maada!

Yet how lovely she was in the cloak! Its blue-green elegance seemed to heighten the fairness and rosiness of her cheeks as the painted folds opened to reveal the inner black fur; its iridescent discs caught the sunlight, enhancing the glisten of her matching earrings. Accenting the color of cloak and canoe hat, a blue-green pattern banded her fringed doeskin shift. And worthy of her own magnificence, Maada's dark eyes betrayed no tears; her perfect teeth flashed in a smile. She was so beautiful!

And the polished canoe! Yatz's eyes caressed its lines. How gracefully the high prow broke through the waves and spread the waters to let the sleek hull glide through! Muscles rippled over twelve naked backs as twelve long painted paddles flashed in rhythmic unison.

Flawless perfection! Truly, there was nothing in all the world so proud and handsome as a Haida canoe carrying a Haida princess.

A few more summers came and went in Hiellen. Each left the village filled to lavishness with the harvest of the sea and the seashore. Abundance freed the people for participation in the fun and splendors of the winter ceremonies; for in their feast-house arts—singing, dancing, and storytelling—the Haida were as vigorous as their bracing winds, as colorful as their sunsets. Abundance made good their boast that in a Haida village, even a slave ate well.

Suddenly, winter gatherings throbbed with excited rumors.

Flying canoes had been seen again! And Iron Men were not supernatural, the rumors said.

They were real men, eager to trade their iron for sea otter pelts. Any man could have iron for his fishing, hunting, and woodworking tools. A woman could have iron for her cooking pots.

But when?

Every eye began to scan the ocean in expectation. Every spare storage chest began to fill with dark, glossy fur, ready for barter.

On July 2nd, 1787, when Haiias and Yatz were again visiting K'yuusdaa, Captain Dixon sailed the *Queen Charlotte* into a bay that lay west of the village, beyond the point. In half an hour of trading, he bought three hundred sea otter cloaks and pelts at one chisel for every skin.

"Cloak Bay!" he proclaimed it joyously, gloating over his wealth in furs. "Queen Charlotte's Islands!" he named Haida Gwaii, after his English queen. Then he turned his eyes southward, along the Haida coast. More furs would be waiting for him. And, obviously, no rival traders.

It was with mixed emotions that Yatz watched the *Queen Charlotte* sail away. Mainly, he felt let down. His own greatest adventure had not been supernatural after all, though the axe-head had power, he knew; he felt that power in his fingers.

"Maada will see the Iron Men, too," he said to Haiias. "Perhaps they'll visit Koyah's village." They had not landed at K'yuusdaa, though the people had all enticed them. That was a disappointment. It was more than a disappointment. "It was an affront," he declared. "The Iron Men lack good manners."

"But the wind and tide were against them," Haiias protested mildly. Above all a skillful seaman, he had been fascinated by the gigantic flying canoe. He had hovered alertly while the *Queen Charlotte* had lowered her whaleboat and her jolly boat to tow her away from a rocky headland. It had been the most exhilarating day of his exhilarating life. "They could do nothing against the tide rip," he reminded his fellow Eagle.

"Except wait," Yatz suggested crisply. The brusqueness of the men had angered him. Trading demanded courtesies. It was not something people accomplished with unseemly haste. Still, he fondled his new chisels. When the trading gave you iron for your woodworking tools, it was not a bad thing. His eyes grew soft and filled with an artist's glow. Once his fingers became accustomed to the new tools, what might he not carve with iron?

First of all, he decided, he would fashion a fish club for Maada's little son—the boy who would come some day to Hiellen as he himself had come. Maada's child, a Sdast'a·aas

25

Saang gaahl Eagle like herself, was her brother's heir, not her husband's.

Yatz's wistful thoughts were on his tiny heir as he watched the *Queen Charlotte* fade into a summer sea mist. He scarcely heard Haiias speaking.

"Sails," Haiias was saying reverently. "Sails to catch the wind and let it push them across the water!"

The *Queen Charlotte* sailed southward through summer fogs, rain, and sunshine. Again and again she stood off the Haida coast to barter for sea otter skins. And she found people avid for things other than iron chisels. They gleefully took tin kettles, brass pans, pewter basins, knives, and buckles. Always, like the people at Cloak Bay, they tried to entice the Iron Men to their villages.

White men were too wary to be caught like that. "Go to their ruddy village? And 'ave them cannibals eat us!" one seaman said to another. They kept suspicious eyes on every Haida who came near them.

On July 24th, the morning fog blew away to reveal sea lions and whales cavorting in sparkling waters. And suddenly 180 men, women, and children were swarming around the sailing ship in canoes. The women and children were boggle-eyed with wonder. The men were hugely enjoying their families' amazement; they had been near the *Queen Charlotte* the day before, trading every last fur they could lay hands on.

White men smiled happily too, until they saw that the Haida had brought no furs. "They 'aven't nothink to trade today," a seaman noted in disgust.

"Today," Captain Dixon echoed sharply, overhearing the seaman. "But there will be other days and other voyages."

He bowed courteously towards a chief in a magnificent Killer Whale canoe. He smiled at the fellow's stately young chieftainess, a handsome girl in a blue-green cloak and hat. She was delightedly holding up a child whose solemn eyes looked out from between a luxurious fur cape and a small Eagle headdress hung plentifully with ermine skins.

Maada hugged the small body close. And very proudly! She wanted the Iron Men to see clearly how lovely her small boy was. She ran a finger over one round, rosy cheek; she kissed chubby fingers. Then she held him out again. The Iron Men, observing his number of ermine skins, would know what a great prince he was. They would honor him with a gift, even as they had honored his father with a gift when he had traded with them for his hunters the day before.

When they made no move to do so, Koyah took his son from Maada. Standing forward in the canoe, he held the little boy up. Attendants indicated the child's regalia—especially the abundance of ermine skins.

The chief's canoes gathered, waiting.

Captain Dixon beckoned Chief Koyah aboard. And Koyah, after kissing the child triumphantly, handed him to his mother. He agilely gained the ship's deck, where he danced, wafting the feathers of peace and friendship so these strangers would feel no fear.

His people watched.

Captain Dixon spoke courteously with smiles and gestures. He frowned, and looked slightly anxious. But he proffered no gift to this chief who had come without furs to barter.

By and by, the Haida chief climbed angrily down the ladder.

"The ruddy nerve!" one seaman muttered. "Expectin' somethink for nothink!"

Maada stood up again; and her eyes were flashing. "I will go," she announced. Ignoring the gasp of disapproval from the

chief's older wives, she kissed her child fondly and handed him to his father. Then she climbed up the ladder.

For her encounter with the Iron Men, she had covered her body from neck to calf with an elegant, close-fitting shift of softened doeskin, painted and deeply fringed. Gaining the deck, she lowered her eyes modestly. Yet she moved about the ship with the confident grace of a chieftainess. Only her eyes betrayed her intense excitement in all the things she saw; things Yatz must have seen on that long ago day when he had been given the axehead.

Now! What would his heir be given?

She stood on the deck, silent, stately, and gracious. Above her, seagulls and eagles circled; below her, the people waited.

Captain Dixon presented her with beads and ear ornaments. He indicated she was to wear them.

She accepted her gift with grace. And silently waited where she was.

But the chief of the Iron Men was escorting her to the ship's rail, a respectful hand on her elbow. He was handing her gallantly down the ladder.

Then, in growing bafflement, Captain Dixon, master of the *Queen Charlotte,* was watching a scene below him.

The moment Maada stepped into the canoe again, the older wives turned on her. "Going with strange men!" they scolded in high-pitched Haida.

She stared at them, stunned by their accusation. This! After a thousand previous hints about an improper interest in her husband's handsome heir. It was not to be borne! The insult of the accusation! The indignity of public censure! On top of the affront to her little son! It was too much. She clutched her child fiercely to her. And the bitterness of years broke through her stately bearing. Maada burst into tears.

People stared at her in disbelief, then consternation. A

chieftainess! A great Sdast'a·aas Saang gaahl Eagle princess, forgetting her dignity!

Alarmed at his young wife's outburst, Chief Koyah laid a soothing hand on her shoulder. The older wives hovered, abashed now and apologetic.

Maada ignored them all. She swiftly shook off her tears, lifted her head, and seated herself in regal calm. She even inclined her head graciously towards the captain who, for all his iron wonders, was so lacking in good manners that he had failed to honor a Haida prince, a future Chief 7idansuu of Eagle House at Hiellen.

Astounded by the scene, and vaguely disturbed by it, Captain Dixon beckoned to the big canoe. With elaborate courtesy, he handed down a gift of iron chisels and a handful of shiny buttons. Maybe that would please the angry lady.

At last! Maada's smile flashed at him. At last a gift for her little princeling! Graciously she distributed the buttons on her child's behalf to the women in the canoe. Then delightedly she showed her son his chisels.

He moved to bite them; but his mother laughingly stopped him. And the big canoe moved away with all the people chanting, and the other canoes as escort.

Truly, thought Captain Dixon, and the thought surprised the captain, there is nothing more splendid than a Haida canoe carrying a Haida chieftainess.

A second thought made the Haida appear even more splendid to him. They had provided him with the equivalent of $90,000 worth of sea otter skins. A fortune in the 1700s!

It was two years later that the *Lady Washington* arrived in Haida waters.

The *Lady Washington* was from Boston.

The first time she stood off the fortified island in front of Koyah's village, on June 11th, 1789, she was commanded by courteous young Captain Gray, whose senior officer was Captain John Kendrick of the *Columbia,* currently trading elsewhere for the same Boston shipowners.

Chiefs Koyah and Skulkin nagaas traded with Captain Gray for their people. Now experienced traders, they demanded clothing as well as metals and trinkets, a request that caught the Boston men unprepared.

Eager for the fabulous furs, however, seamen offered the very shirts off their backs. And so, unwittingly, they started a new rivalry in the village. Every man desired a garment made of the cloth that was so much finer than the material Haida women made from shredded cedar bark.

Unfortunately, seamen could spare no more shirts when the *Lady Washington* came back again during the same trading voyage.

This second time she anchored off Koyah's village, the *Lady Washington* was under the command of Captain Kendrick, who had handed his bigger ship *Columbia* over to Captain Gray.

Captain Kendrick was a huge man with reddish hair and an unreasonable temper. This day he had been drinking. And in spite of anxious protests from his officers, he let the Haida swarm aboard the *Lady Washington,* contrary to the custom. At the same time, he insisted on having his personal laundry hung out on deck to dry. No young whippersnappers were going to tell him how to run his ship! No dirty savages were going to upset his private arrangements!

So, while the chiefs bartered, the Haida explored the tempting wonders of the Iron Man's canoe. One of them filched a shirt from the captain's laundry and disappeared overboard.

Captain Kendrick was livid when the theft was discovered.

"I'll teach these thieving devils a lesson they'll never forget," he thundered. "Arm every man!"

Muskets bristled on all sides. Warning shots blazed. Seagulls dropped, dead. And fierce warriors trembled.

"Man that gun! . . . FIRE!"

A tree on shore splintered.

Staggered by the power of his thundersticks, the Haida watched Captain Kendrick.

"Grab the chiefs!" he roared, red-faced with fury.

Koyah and Skulkin nagaas were seized. A cannon was dismounted, and a leg of each chief was clamped into the iron mounts.

Shamed eyes turned away from this humiliation of the chiefs; for it was not the Haida way to leap into battle while the odds were hopeless. The wilderness had taught them that only patience assured final victory, that a time always came for boldness. Then you struck without mercy.

Meanwhile, the chiefs' hair was cut off like slaves' hair. Horrified eyes watched this new indignity. The chiefs were further pinioned by ropes around their necks; ship's paint was daubed on their faces; and they were flogged.

Neither chief moved a muscle. But the eyes of both burned with a fire that was never to be quenched. Hatred smouldered in the eyes of every watching Haida, too. But theirs was a patient hatred. They could wait for the right moment for revenge.

"Now!" Captain Kendrick roared at the Haida. "Bring back my shirt or your chiefs will be blasted to bits!"

The shirt was handed up; other pilfered articles appeared as if by magic. At the same time, furs were picked up defiantly.

Even the captain's bleary eyes saw that trading was finished here.

No! It was not finished. Not while he held the chiefs captive.

"Bring me every last skin in the village!" he yelled. "Every last skin, or your chiefs will be killed. Your village will be blown to pieces!"

The Haida understood him. Alert eyes could read the threat of the muskets and the menace of the big guns. They brought every pelt to the ship.

"Now!" Captain Kendrick boasted. "I'll show you how civilized men do things." And to prove what a fair-minded fellow a civilized man was, he paid for every skin at the prevailing rate in chisels.

Then he released the chiefs. And training his guns on the Haida, Captain Kendrick fled from their waters.

Maada was horrified. Almost in disbelief she stared at her husband's shorn head, at the paint on his face, at the welts on his body.

"This is an insult not to be borne!" she declared.

She looked again at his shorn head, shrinking visibly from it. This was the utter stigma, the sign of a social outcast; and welts, unlike the honorable scars of battle, were as vile a stigma.

"*You* were captured. *You* were made a slave by the Iron Men," she whispered, as though needing to convince herself that this dreadful thing could be true. "*You* were ridiculed."

Her towering pride was shattered. Chief Koyah, her husband, had been utterly humiliated. Word would spread through Haida Gwaii; and wherever he moved, people would turn their heads away not to see his humiliation; chiefs would turn their heads away also, and not seat him in the old, honored places.

The very name itself, Koyah, had been dishonored. It had been degraded among the proud, ancient Haida names. Her eyes chanced on Chisalgas, who was destined to wear the name next. Hero of a dozen raids, the young chieftain was heir now only to a bitter shame.

Maada's eyes sought her son. Even he was shamed. Only blood could wipe out a shame such as this.

"This is an insult not to be borne!" she said again.

"The insult will be wiped out," Koyah fiercely assured her.

"It will be wiped out in blood," Koyah's heir vowed.

But all in good time.

Haida revenge could be patient. Patient, but sure. Sure as the turning of the tide. Sure as the coming of the winter gales.

———

On the sixteenth day of June, in the year '91, Captain Kendrick anchored again off Koyah's village. Having taught these "thieving devils" a lesson, he felt little fear of them. Too, he had changed his ship's rig in China. The savages might not even recognize the *Lady Washington*. And if they did, they would see that she was even more strongly armed now. In any case, he was getting furs even here. "And to blazes with everybody!" Captain Kendrick was once more in liquor.

Drunk too with dreams of a private fur-trading empire, Captain Kendrick had disobeyed his owners' orders. He had not returned to Boston. Now he ignored his officers' warnings about the number of visitors. Customarily, only chiefs boarded a ship to trade for their people.

"Oh, let the devils come!" he said. "They know who's master here."

He had taught them a lesson. And just as he had expected, the curs were slinking back to lick the boots that had kicked them. Even old Koyah was here with furs, as though nothing had ever happened.

Captain Kendrick greeted him affably. He was merely relieved that the old boy did not perform his usual dance and shake out those foolish feathers. He gallantly saluted Koyah's chieftainess in the canoe below. In spite of the labret in her lower lip, she was a handsome wench, he thought, sitting in the folds of a fur-lined blue-green cloak. Haida women really decked themselves. Her fringed doeskin shift was ornamented with bracelets and anklets and earrings. He winked at her in admiration. And he cheerfully allowed fifty Haida onto the ship. He even let twelve come onto the quarterdeck to watch his bartering with Chief Koyah.

His officers were less cheerful. They did not like the look of the Haida men circling the *Lady Washington* in canoes.

Nor did a gunner like it. He predicted to a mate that muskets would be broken out. "Muskets!" He clapped a hand to his head. He and his fellow gunners had been overhauling arms on the quarterdeck. The arms chests were closed, but unlocked. The keys were still standing in them. He hurried to warn the captain. "Captain, sir!"

Captain Kendrick whirled on the gunner, furious at the interruption. He struck him a savage blow; pushed him off the quarterdeck.

Koyah's quick eyes had caught the gesture towards the arms chests. And when the captain turned back to trade, he found the Haida around the arms chests. The keys had vanished.

Quick as a fish, Chief Koyah leapt on the chests. And standing with a bare foot on each, he taunted the careless captain. "Now put me in your gun carriage!" he yelled out in savage triumph.

Captain Kendrick did not know the Haida tongue. But he did understand the daggers that glinted in a dozen places. He understood the marlinespike held menacingly above him. And he understood the ferocious war chant that rose on all sides of the *Lady Washington.*

Then he saw the young chieftainess in the bow of his ship.

She stood like an avenging goddess.

In Maada the blood of a thousand Haida chiefs throbbed

with the fierce war chant; the spirit of the mighty Sdast'a·aas Saang gaahl Eagles soared.

Her quick eyes scanned the daggers, ready if Koyah should give the word. But he had a plan more ambitious than the swift death of the Iron Men, she knew. He would wipe out his shame with a victory unprecedented in Haida legend.

He would capture the ship. He had captured the ship already; for, deprived of their thundersticks, the Iron Men were merely mortal. And what mortals were a match for the Haida?

His people would loot the ship to let Koyah give a potlatch so rich in gifts that taunts would be stilled forever. And that was not all! He would take the Iron Men captive. And before he killed the chief of the Iron Men under his totem pole at the potlatch, Koyah would cut off his hair, tie a rope around his neck, paint his face, and have the slaves flog him—the pale-faced slaves! Pale-faced slaves would serve the guests at Koyah's potlatch. And then? Then the crowning glory! Where other chiefs burned a small canoe in their feasthouses to show their wealth, Koyah would burn the flying canoe before the eyes of the assembled chiefs and their people. All would witness his unprecedented triumph. All: Gannyaa . . . Cumshewa . . . Skidegate . . . 7idansuu . . .

And then, after such glory, who would dare to breathe the name Koyah without respect?

It was an ambitious plan. Maada saw that her husband's eyes already glittered with thoughts of his coming status. Still, he did not give the word to seize the chief of the Iron Men. She frowned, watching him. Why was her husband waiting?

After a year of bitterness, Koyah was savoring the first moments of sweet revenge. He was playing with his victim, taunting him with the keys of the arms chests; for without their thundersticks, the Iron Men were helpless.

She saw that the chief of the Iron Men was entreating with

him, offering him lavish trade goods in return for the precious keys. He was offering even his own coat with shiny buttons. His own hat! And all the time he was edging towards a companion-way. But men stood ready to stop him.

Meanwhile, she saw, the plan was proceeding nicely. Warriors were forcing Iron Men below to hold them captive in the cabins; they were returning to the deck with booty. They were joyously hailing the village, waving clothing and copper kettles.

What she did not see was that officers were slipping into their own cabins below, where their private arms were waiting; that officers were gathering, well armed, at the companionway near the captain. What she did not know was that the captain's words meant, "Wait until I shout 'Follow me!' "

Suddenly she sensed the tensing of the situation.

Then she saw the explosion.

Koyah jumped off the chests. His dagger ripped the captain's jacket.

The captain yelled, "FOLLOW ME!" He grabbed a musket and fired it. He led a charge of officers, all firing pistols.

The little gunner shouted, and flung open the unlocked arms chests. Muskets hurtled into waiting fingers.

Alarm raced through the ship.

At the first musket shot, the Haida wavered. Their own ignorance panicked them. They knew they no longer faced fellow mortals; for thundersticks had a mystic power. They remembered that Iron Men were not mere human beings. How could they be human men, this people without wives and children? You could only flee, they knew, as you fled from Kali Koustli. You could not fight an unseen power.

Maada saw the retreat beginning.

"Stand! Fight!" she urged. "Or you will be shamed forever."

Chisalgas leapt with his dagger. A musket dropped him, dead. A dozen fell dead around him.

"Stand! Fight!" Maada yelled. She felt fire burn through her thigh, but still she urged them. A knife slashed her cheek. Then a man jumped towards her. His cutlass flashed. It slashed off her left arm, with its glory of copper bracelets. Blood gushed from her. Yet she cried, "FIGHT!"

But the rout was complete by this time. Dead bodies lay everywhere, Haida bodies. Wounded men fled the ship in panic, pursued by the deadly muskets.

The chieftainess, the last living Haida on the ship, tumbled into the water. She raised her right arm to swim, but a hail of shot spat around her. And Maada died in the sea.

A fire of muskets and cannons raked the water. Armed boats were launched, with orders to seek out and kill survivors. Yet many Haida escaped.

Maada's small son was not one of them. He was killed where he stood screaming on the dreadful beach.

Somehow, Koyah escaped from the muskets.

But he could not escape from a sacred duty, his duty to his dead people. For, until they were avenged, their ghosts would hover in the air, unable to travel along the trail to the Land of Souls. The Haida blood code demanded now that he avenge all his dead relatives.

For every Haida slain, an Iron Man must die. Any Iron Man!

Unaware of this blood code, the triumphant seamen on the *Lady Washington* sang their new boasting ballad:

The number killed upon our deck that day was sixty good,
And full as many wounded as soon we understood.

Actually, more than a hundred were killed that day. And for every Haida slain, an Iron Man must die.

Any Iron Man!

39

T H R E E

YATZ WAS DESOLATED BY WORD OF THE TRAGEDY at Koyah's village. His lovely sister was dead, and his heir too.

Until their deaths had been avenged, their ghosts must hover unhappily near the place where they had been killed. Yet he could not further shame Koyah by taking the revenge out of his hands; not when Maada had died trying to lift that shame from her husband.

He rejoiced when word finally came that Koyah had captured and burned a sailing ship, killing the entire crew of Iron Men.

Now, many ghosts had been set free. But not yet all! The fate of two ghosts still haunted Yatz. Perhaps it would be left to him, after all, to avenge his heir and his sister. Perhaps he would be the one to encounter that cruelest of all chiefs, Kendrick. His eyes narrowed and glinted with awful purpose.

Revenge was a sacred duty.

Fortunately for Captain Kendrick's peace of mind, he did not concern himself with what "savages" thought. He did not even concern himself unduly with what his shipowners thought.

His dream was of a permanent fur-trading post for himself and for the two sons he had brought to the North Pacific. He was negotiating for a site on the west coast of Vancouver Island, south of the Queen Charlotte Islands. And while Captain Gray sailed the *Columbia* back to Boston, Captain Kendrick stayed on in the Pacific as if the *Lady Washington* were his own ship. His son John had left him to go into the service of Spain; but John would be back. His son Solomon had sailed with the *Columbia;* but he would be back also.

And in fact, Solomon Kendrick did not linger in Boston. He quickly shipped out again for the northwest coast, sailing as second mate on another ship, the *Jefferson.*

Commanded by Josiah Roberts, the *Jefferson* rounded the Horn and made first for the South Seas, where she picked up 13,000 seal skins at the St. Ambrose Islands. Wintering at the Marquesas, they laid the keel and built the schooner whose frame they had carried in their hold. Solomon Kendrick was made first officer of this schooner, the *Resolution,* a speedy little sailer.

Cap'n Roberts provisioned the slower *Jefferson* at the Sandwich (Hawaiian) Islands and steered for North America. He made his landfall south of Gray's River (Columbia River), where the scarcity of furs sent him scudding north, along the west coast of Vancouver Island, to meet his schooner.

At Nootka, on the west side of the island, he found the *Resolution* riding at anchor with several rival trading ships, including the *Lady Washington*. He heard lively rumors.

"Plenty of skins north," an English skipper assured him, "but keep an eye on those Haida. They're treacherous devils." They had made a completely unprovoked attack on one vessel, he said, burning her and killing her crew. Too, they were arrogant. They were no longer content with chisels. Now they demanded muskets and powder for their pelts, or cloth, or thick sheets of copper, or moose hides. The hides were for making armor. "They're bloody warlike!" he said. "Still, they have plenty of prime sea otter."

Cap'n Roberts scowled at the news. He had plenty of chisels.

He still had plenty of chisels when the trading season was over. Chisels could not compete with the cloth offered by English rivals. Time after time he saw piles of prime skins; but the Haida refused his chisels.

Cap'n Roberts was not licked, however. Being a shrewd Yankee trader, he could swap around a little. He remembered herds of elk in the region of Gray's River. He would barter iron there for elk hides; then he'd trade the hides for sea otter.

He dispatched the *Resolution* to Gray's River. But the native people there did not want iron either, not unless it came in the shape of four-foot-long swords, or neck rings. They parted with only twenty-seven elk hides.

"Blast them!" said Cap'n Roberts.

But he was not beaten.

Wintering south of Nootka, he set all hands to work. While the men yearned for the sunshine and fresh fruit of the South Seas, they burned charcoal and helped the smith fashion four-foot-long swords, and neck rings, and daggers. They burned mussel shells for lime to tan hides. They acquired a few furs, and 160 fathoms of dentalium shells, or native money. They also put the ships into good order.

By the end of March, the ships were in better shape than

the men; they were ready for the trading season. The *Jefferson* would go north to do what she could with what she had, while the speedier *Resolution* returned to Gray's River to barter for hides.

"If you can't get enough hides, Captain Burling, go on to California and get something!" Cap'n Roberts ordered. "We'll meet at Cloak Bay if you don't overhaul me before that."

With sea otter breeding grounds located near Cloak Bay, he knew that K'yuusdaa's sea hunters would have stores of prime pelts. He thought he could manage to keep them dickering with him until the *Resolution* arrived with the elk hides.

There was a delay, getting started. A canoe disappeared from the *Resolution*.

"Those thieving devils!" said Captain Burling; and he sent young Mr. Kendrick in an armed whaleboat to the nearest native village.

There, with muskets and swivel gun trained on the cedar houses, Mr. Kendrick demanded the stolen canoe.

Sure enough, the villagers produced it.

Mr. Kendrick scowled. "They need another lesson or two along this coast," he muttered. "FIRE!" he ordered his crew.

Three native men dropped dead on the beach. Two fell wounded. The rest fled into the forest.

"We'll give them a good taste of the medicine while we're at it," the officer decided.

His men ransacked the deserted village, taking stores of dried fish, chisels, copper, muskets, and powder. They smashed several houses. They took the six best canoes and broke up others. Then they returned to the *Resolution* and wrote up the incident triumphantly in the log. They had done a great day's work in civilizing a savage coast. They meant to have it remembered.

"The dirty devils!" said young Mr. Kendrick as he sailed south to Gray's River in the *Resolution*. "They won't forget that in a hurry."

They would not, indeed!

Meanwhile, the *Jefferson* moved northward through waters alive with whales and porpoises. She traded warily along the Haida coast, dropping anchor finally in Cloak Bay on May 19th, 1794.

Cap'n Roberts found K'yuusdaa almost deserted. The few people remaining in the village were busy. Several men were smoothing a fragrant cedar log. Others were working over a gigantic cedar Bear sculpture, meticulously fitting pieces of abalone mother-of-pearl into the teeth, eyes, nostrils, and ears of the stylized beast. Still other men were massing firewood. Women were smoking clams and spring salmon. Only one old, old lady seemed to have time to train her piercing eyes on the Iron Men.

No one produced a pelt. All, however, indicated that the villagers would soon be returning from Alaskan waters.

The brisk Yankee found things to do. "Set the hands to brewing spruce beer, Mr. McGee," he ordered. "We have to clean up this scurvy."

"Aye, aye, sir." The first officer of the *Jefferson* moved off, and he stepped lively.

Hiellen's sea hunters had followed the seal and the sea otter far to the north. Their families were near them, camped on the outer islands.

Other members of the village were visiting the Alaskan Haida, the Kaigani, on state affairs. Yatz was with this group.

His uncle, Chief 7idansuu, had been lost at sea the previous summer; and Yatz was to formally assume the name and the chieftainship. His claims must be made and witnessed publicly at a potlatch. Kaigani chiefs must be among the witnesses.

But first, a potlatch was to take place almost immediately at K'yuusdaa, where a memorial pole was being readied. It was a plain, stout pole topped by a Grizzly Bear, a Raven crest.

As soon as the sea hunters were ready to return to Haida Gwaii, they joined the Kaigani potlatch party; and a magnificent company of Eagles and Ravens started south together at the end of May. They divided their families among eighty canoes, in the Haida way, to bind the whole fleet together in case of peril out on the ocean.

With long, long, sunny days, May can be glorious in northern waters. The day they set out from the Alaskan island, the world was blue and white. The sky was blue, with white clouds. The mountains were blue, with glistening snow peaks reflected in deep, cold water. The sea was blue: blue with white surf, white shell-strewn beaches, and white seagulls flashing in the sun.

Yatz fondly watched his little daughter hugging her doll in the canoe next to his. Her eyes sparkled like the wet brown kelp bulbs that bobbed in the sea swells about her. Her hair streamed out below her Killer Whale canoe hat. Earrings glinted. Rosy cheeks shone with skin grease that had been smudged with charcoal below her eyes to protect them from the glare. She was a precious princess! She carried a noble Raven bloodline and she would mother Kaigani chiefs some day.

Since the Haida fleet approached K'yuusdaa from the northeast, Yatz did not see the *Jefferson* lying at anchor in Cloak Bay. He did notice Iron Men near the bonfires and torches on the beach. But at the moment they were unimportant.

The important thing was a proper welcome to the Alaskan

visitors. With approval he noted that blackened slaves rushed into the surf to cast copper shields under the canoes of the greatest chiefs; while, magnificent in his regalia, an ancient but honored K'yuusdaa chief danced on the beach, shaking his bird rattle, and wafting the swan's-down of peace and friendship from his crown of sea lion bristles. Drums were beating; people were chanting on shore and in the canoes; paddles were dipping in ceremonial precision. A great occasion had started, appropriately.

Again, it was only the old, old lady who was not too busy to observe those around her. She turned her piercing eyes, now, on Yatz. "There is something," she hinted. Listening to the Iron Men, she had discovered something.

Yatz waited respectfully to learn what the aged chieftainess had discovered.

One flying canoe was here, she informed him; another flying canoe was coming. "And one of the chiefs on the coming canoe has a hated name."

"Kendrick?" His Haida tongue made it Kendghick.

"Kendrick." She nodded, and watched him closely.

He looked at the surf. But he neither saw it nor heard it. He saw only a little boy screaming on a beach; he heard only a small ghost wailing over Koyah's village. "I knew it was being left to me to avenge my heir," he muttered as though to himself. "When Kendrick comes, I will kill him."

Cap'n Roberts watched the arrival of the Haida with growing enthusiasm. It was not the magnificence of the chiefs that impressed him so much as the magnificence of the sea otter skins being lifted from the canoes. There were hundreds and hundreds of them, many five and six feet long. Prime pelts.

"Smoke and oakum!" he exclaimed.

He had made shrewd use of his waiting time, apart from brewing spruce beer. He had learned a few Haida words and had made friends in the village. He had especially ingratiated himself with the woodworkers by bringing a ship's carpenter, "Chips," ashore with a plane to speed the smoothing of the cedar log. He had further pleased them by his genuine, and by no means silent, amazement at the skill and artistry displayed on house posts and totem poles and on utensils. He had not found it necessary to admit that the towering, grotesque figures unnerved him somewhat, especially in a half-light.

Obviously the smoothed log was going to be planted in the waiting hole; obviously the enormous mother-of-pearl-encrusted Bear was going to be placed on top. "But I wonder how in thunder they'll haul the thing up," he commented to Mr. McGee. More than eager to establish good relations, he invited the village carvers aboard the *Jefferson;* he demonstrated to them the virtues of civilized man's block and tackle; he indicated that he would be pleased to send equipment to the village.

"More than pleased!" he assured his first mate. "This place is an El Dorado." His eyes sparkled, then frowned. When would the *Resolution* turn up with those hides? And how was he going to keep these villagers on his hook until his schooner got here? Rival traders might sail into Cloak Bay any minute with tempting cloth.

Something had to be done!

Cap'n Roberts started trading; and for once a Yankee encouraged the Haida to palaver as long as they liked. He disposed of some chisels, daggers, and neck rings. Then, in desperation, he began stripping the *Jefferson*. He swapped a swivel for two skins, cabin curtains for two, a Japanese flag for one, a tablecloth and several bed sheets for one pelt apiece. And he kept scowling across the sea. "When is that blamed schooner going to get here?" he mumbled.

More canoes came alongside with beautiful sea otter skins.

"Give them anything but the galley stove!" he ordered. "Break out the old sails, Mr. McGee. They'll always take cloth." His eyes lit with a notion. "Maybe they'll take chests, too. Set Chips to making chests, Mr. McGee!"

"Aye, aye, sir."

But cloth was best, he knew. "See if the hands have any old clothes they want to sell, Mr. McGee. And . . ." His eyes really lit up this time. "And set them to making women's shifts out of the old sails, Mr. McGee!"

"Petticoats . . . sir?" The mate looked exceedingly doubtful.

"Petticoats, Mr. McGee! All hands making petticoats. And put some ginger into them, Mr. McGee!"

"Aye . . . aye . . . sir. Aye, aye, sir!" Mr. McGee stepped lively.

"I'll be hanged if I'll make petticoats," one of the hands grumbled.

"You'll be hanged if you don't," said Cap'n Roberts, overhearing. "Tell them to stow the gaff, Mr. McGee. There's to be no easing off until the job's done."

"Aye, aye, sir."

Where was the *Resolution?*

All the while, the potlatch was progressing to an important moment. The pole was about to be raised; and at the head chief's invitation, Cap'n Roberts took two spare topmasts and some tackle to the village.

As the Haida watched in wonder, a few Yankee seamen raised the thick, heavy pole.

Head Chief Gannyaa was delighted. He invited the *Jefferson's* chiefs to a feast where they were publicly thanked and presented with a sea otter skin each.

Yatz was not delighted with the innovation. "It was better when we raised the pole ourselves," he told his wife. "When the men had to lift, and push the props under; and when the

49

women and children had to pull on the ropes, they liked it better. They cheered twice as joyously when the job was finished."

Cap'n Roberts was concerned by Yatz's obvious disapproval. He singled out the frowning young man to assure him that a ship was coming soon with great piles of hides.

The frown did not lift. In fact, for one alarming moment, it seemed to the Yankee that the Haida looked murderous.

It made him uneasy. You could never trust these bloodthirsty Haida, he knew. They thought nothing of making an unprovoked attack on a white man, or on his ship. Like their totem poles, they were more than a mite unnerving.

Where was the *Resolution?*

On June 13th, there had been word that a ship was sighted. Nothing had turned up, not even a rival trader.

By July 8th, Cap'n Roberts was desperate. When he and his equipment were again invited to the village, this time to hoist the Bear, he was thankful for the diversion. More than thankful! "I'm dee-lighted to be of service to the owners of fifteen hundred prime sea otter pelts, Mr. McGee," he said.

After raising the Bear, he and his party went on to the town chief's house by invitation. Spryly he climbed in through a front door that was a hole in a terrifying totem pole. Inside, he was struck still. "Great wailing williwaughs!" he whispered, awed.

There were at least six hundred guests and spectators in the gigantic cedar house. Excavations had permitted a series of smoothly planked terraces to lead down to an enormous fire under the smoke hole. An oval hearth was white with broken clamshells. Light from the blazing fire flickered on carved house posts, on crest-painted screens, on decorated storage boxes on the highest gallery, and on a colorful company. Men in dancing regalia and bird masks cast fantastic shadows. Box drums throbbed. People chanted.

Gifts were brought forth, displayed, and then piled into a mound: war garments, sea otter cloaks, iron neck rings, copper necklaces and bracelets and anklets, glistening abalone earrings . . .

The horde of spectators was dismissed.

Only chiefs and important women were seated in careful order on cedar mats around the blazing fire. Majestic in cloaks and headdresses, they solemnly had witnessed the pole-raising; they graciously accepted gifts for this public service.

Cap'n Roberts as graciously accepted five prime sea otter pelts for his participation in the ceremonies.

Next day he lapsed back into waiting.

Where was the *Resolution?*

He had had frequent visits from one great sea-hunting chief, Haiias.

Haiias was enchanted with the *Jefferson;* he never ceased considering her sails.

Now Cap'n Roberts said to him, "Chief! Why don't we fit your canoe out with sails?" He set his men to work; and he was so well paid by the wildly happy sea hunter that he might have gone into the sail-installing business had he not already used up every spare stitch of canvas making garments for women. He sailed with Haiias, explaining that without a keel, he could do little more than run before the wind.

Running before the wind was sheer joy to Haiias.

"Happy as a clam at low tide, Mr. McGee," the captain reported. He wished he were as happy.

On July 17th, the *Phoenix* arrived from Bengal with cloth. While she swung at anchor for eleven days, the *Jefferson* could not secure one pelt.

On August 1st, the English ship *Jenny* dropped anchor in Cloak Bay. She had news of the *Resolution.* Captain Adamson had seen her beating her way north just before a gale had hit the southern tip of the Queen Charlotte Islands on May 15th. He thought she must have been caught by it. It had been one of the ninety-mile-an-hour gales that sometimes lash the southern tip of the Charlottes. Such a sea had risen, Captain Adamson said, that ships lying in harbor had rolled yardarm and yardarm in the water. The schooner could not have survived it. She must have gone down with all hands.

"God rest their souls!" muttered a shocked Cap'n Roberts. He was licked. At last!

"Have all the skins out to be cleaned, aired, and repacked, Mr. McGee," he ordered.

Masts and yards were examined, wood and water taken aboard. "Well," he announced on August 16th, "we're bung up and bilge free, and we'll sail as soon as it freshens."

Just before the *Jefferson* sailed out of Cloak Bay in company with the *Jenny,* Cap'n Roberts was astounded to have the new Chief 7idansuu come out to the ship with Haiias to wish him a safe journey. "And hanged if I don't think those savages looked sorry for me, Mr. McGee," he commented, baffled. "I guess there's no figuring out these Haida."

He had no way of knowing that a canoe, also, had brought word of the *Resolution.*

Haida intelligence was more accurate than the *Jenny's.*

The *Resolution* had not foundered in a gale. She had run into a harbor for shelter. And there, with Chief Cumshewa, the ever-watchful Koyah had captured her. The two chiefs had burned the *Resolution* with the decapitated bodies of all but one of her crew on board.

One last man had been discovered hiding in a cask. He had been taken to the village to serve as a slave.

Yatz, the new Chief 7idansuu, was infinitely relieved by this news. At last he felt sure that Maada's ghost and her small son's ghost had escaped to the happy Land of Souls. And he knew that their spirits would return some day; he would watch every new baby until he recognized those loved spirits again.

Too, revenge was no longer his sacred duty. He need not kill. "My heart feels good!" he told Haiias. "Come along the trail," he invited his old comrade when they had returned to the village from the ship. "There's so much to talk of. Life changes so swiftly these days."

Head Chief Gannyaa had decided to migrate north to the Alaskan islands, as so many Haida had already done. Haiias would go with him. They would throw in their lot with the Kaigani.

In consequence, the new Chief 7idansuu would now be head chief of the Sdast'a·aas Eagles in Haida Gwaii. He would be responsible for people all along the north coast of Haida Gwaii.

"These are great times," Haiias said to him when they stood again where they had once stood as boys, near the northwestern tip of the largest island of the Haida group.

A bracing wind lifted their hair. Sunlight brightened the Eagle crests tattooed on their lithe but full-chested bodies. It glinted on their copper armbands as they stood scanning the wild coast that stretched away to the southwest.

A sadly depleted herd of sea otters swam towards the old rookery. Several climbed warily up on the rocks. One lifted his head in alarm. All slid into the water. And then, after a few minutes of waiting, they ventured timidly again towards the rocks. But an eagle screeched; and they went scurrying seaward, making fast for protecting kelp beds awash out in the ocean.

Yatz shook his head, watching them. "They are so frightened now, Haiias," he said. "So changed. Do you remember them that day I first came here?"

A seagull caught Haiias's attention before he could answer. It swooped to the sea near a rocky headland, and rose again with a fish.

An eagle shrieked and plummeted.

The gull dropped the fish.

The eagle caught the dropped fish before it could hit the water.

"The eagle!" exclaimed Haiias.

Yatz's eyes, too, were shining. The swiftness of an eagle always thrilled him. That, and the leap of a salmon. "What superb creatures we have all around us!" he said reverently. Then once again his eyes sought the sea otters. They were so very human! And so frightened now! As frightened as a small boy on a beach when muskets blazed.

Haiias dropped an affectionate hand on his shoulder.

"These are exciting times!" he said. "And you will be a great chief now, little brother." He grinned at the old term of endearment.

"I will be a great chief," Yatz agreed; and his quiet voice rang with purpose.

F O U R

NOW THAT HE WAS CHIEF 7IDANSUU, Yatz was lord of one mighty family, overlord of a dozen others; and family was an encompassing term in Haida Gwaii.

Like a Haida house, a Haida family held large numbers of people together. Family affection, the central fire, warmed countless cousins, aunts, uncles, grandparents, and in-laws as well as father, mother, sisters, brothers. Family responsibility—the strong posts, beams, and planks—sheltered the whole kin connection. Family traditions and crests enriched and decorated the entire lineage.

Loyalty was a blood relation; security was a blood alliance. Every child was precious to a hundred people; no outsider would dare to touch him. He was safe even away from his own relatives; for if he wore the Eagle crest, he was descended from Copper Woman, and every Haida Eagle would leap to defend him; if he wore the Raven crest or Killer Whale, he was descended from Foam Woman, and every Haida Raven was his instant champion.

Yet there were smaller, fonder relationships; and few were fonder than that of a chief and his growing nephews. With Chief 7idansuu, this bond became strongest of all between him and the third of his four nephews.

When Maada and her son died, a younger sister's two tiny boys became the 7idansuu heirs. Through the years, several daughters were born to this sister's family. Later, there was a third son, Gwaii gang·hling, and then a fourth son.

By the time Gwaii gang·hling was born in 1812, his two older brothers were almost men. By the time he went visiting the villages with his uncle in 1817, they were married to 7idansuu's daughters in the traditional pattern of heirs apparent. Gwaii gang·hling was then five years old. His uncle (Yatz) was forty-six.

It was a brisk, sunny day in August 1817 when uncle and nephew stood together on the beach at Massett. Massett was a large village on the northern coast of Haida Gwaii, near the mouth of the biggest inlet.

The chief was telling the little boy the sad story of his mother Maada. (In the Haida way, Gwaii gang·hling called his mother's Eagle sister "Mother Maada." It was his father's Raven sister he addressed as "Aunt.")

7idansuu told him how Mother Maada and her son had died, and how their ghosts had been freed by Koyah's revenge. Koyah had burned one ship and killed its crew, he said; then he had burned another ship and killed its crew also, including wicked

Chief Kendrick. "And Koyah was himself killed the year after that," he told the boy. The shamed chief had died attacking yet another ship in yet another desperate bid to regain standing among the chiefs.

"And that was the end of the story," said Gwaii gang·hling. Like any sensitive child, he was eager to have a sadness finished, and everyone living happily ever after.

"No, that was not the end of the story." Chief 7idansuu's eyes sought a ten-year-old lad playing catch on the beach. "Koyah left a heritage of shame to his family, especially to his nephews and his nephews' nephews."

"Like Skawal?" the little boy asked. His eyes were wide with anxiety as he, too, turned to watch his favorite cousin.

Happily playing catch, Skawal tossed a wooden V to another boy, who caught it deftly on a polished stick and hurled it back again. After a brisk rally, Skawal missed the V, so his opponent rushed up to pull his hair. He resisted the penalty in a laughing tussle. Then he leapt up, grinning, eager to win a chance at retaliation. He tossed the V again and again until his opponent missed, and Skawal was pulling his hair.

Gwaii gang·hling clapped his hands and giggled.

7idansuu did not look so happy.

Skawal's mother was a chieftainess in Koyah's line, and her son's future troubled her. As she was 7idansuu's sister-in-law, it also concerned the head chief of the Sdast'a·aas Eagles. With the Haida pattern of family responsibility, his younger brother's son was his son also. Yet the boy was not his to help! He was not a Sdast'a·aas Eagle.

In six or seven years, Skawal should leave Eagle House at Hiellen to go to live with his mother's Raven relatives in Koyah's village. But what future was there for him in a shamed lodge? The chief sighed deeply, thinking about it.

Gwaii gang·hling glanced up with quick sympathy. "I'll play catch with you," he offered, in affectionate concern for his uncle's unhappiness.

Chief 7idansuu caught his breath, glancing down at the little fellow. This child was his lost heir, returned from the Land of Souls. He had the same eyes, the same lively look of Maada.

He laid a fond hand on the small, naked shoulder. Having two older brothers, Gwaii gang·hling was not his uncle's heir; but he was his uncle's favorite. The chief delighted in his merry yet sensitive ways. He loved to take him on trips like this, visiting the villages. When he took Gwaii gang·hling, though, he often took Skawal as well. In fact, he made a point of showing public favor to the boy who was shadowed by Koyah's shame.

Naturally, Gwaii gang·hling's older brothers were dear to 7idansuu, also. Daring sea hunters and slave raiders, they were as exuberant as Haiias had been. He sometimes looked at them with a rush of yearning for his old comrade, who was now a troubled Kaigani chief wearing the ancient name of Gannyaa. He admired and respected and loved his two sons-in-law. But he sensed that only Gwaii gang·hling was like himself. He would be the artist.

By instinct, the child's grubby fingers were now appreciating the smoothness of the canoe near him; his eyes were following the strong lines of the Killer Whale on its high prow.

The artist in the man responded. "See how he's made to fit the shape," he said, sweeping his arm along the mythological supernatural Whale. "His head is squeezed in here . . . And see how his dorsal fin's pressed back here!"

"What . . . if he . . . whoomps out?" the child suggested, wide eyed.

"Yes! What!" There was that feeling of suppressed power. And the child had caught it. The pleased chief traced out one repeated shape with a finger. It was an oval that had been almost, but not quite, flattened along four sides. It was a strong shape that was here an eye, there the joint of a mighty tail fluke. Again and again in the design, some part of the Killer Whale had been abstracted into this boxed oval. This distinctive motif was basic; a young artist would have to learn it. It was the ovoid or "eye form" that so beautifully patterned storage boxes and Chilkat blankets. He traced it, and traced it in silence.

"I'll paint the Killer Whale on all my canoes," declared Gwaii gang·hling grandly.

"He's not our crest to use," his uncle reminded him gently. "Don't you like the Eagle for your canoes? Or the Frog?"

"I like the Eagle lots better than old Killer Whale," the boy announced, with instant scorn for the previously admired decoration. "But—" and he paused, pulled by two loyalties. "But the Killer Whale looks beautiful when he's tattooed on Skawal."

Chief 7idansuu sighed, his thoughts whisked back to Skawal, and Koyah.

Koyah's downfall had shaken all the chiefs. The deterioration of Koyah's village had alarmed 7idansuu and had emphasized for him the terrible responsibility of a hereditary chief. He could do so much harm, for generations.

Shocked by the realization of what shame could do to a Haida chief's people, 7idansuu had redoubled his own efforts with the Sdast'a·aas Eagles. Under his watchful eye, their houses all along the north coast of Haida Gwaii had continued to be well kept, well provisioned, and more and more brilliantly decorated with reminders of their heritage.

"Every one of you is descended from Copper Woman," he reminded his Eagles, pointing to the Frog crest that had come down to them from her. "Every one of you has chief's blood. And chiefs must have only fine things." He scrutinized flawless canoes, patterned storage boxes, and horn spoons that were exquisite, miniature totem poles. He encouraged people to be haughty in their dealings with white traders. "Demand quality trade goods from them," he urged. "Remember that you shame the sea otters when you accept inferior goods in return for their beautiful fur blankets. Remember that their ghosts may retaliate if they are offended."

"Not a scrap of humility in the lot," traders complained, scowling at arrogant demands. But they brought out their best woolen cloth for the Sdast'a·aas Eagles. "They're all chiefs," they explained, shrugging with helplessness in face of this dauntless pride.

Pride was the Haida battlement, Chief 7idansuu had decided. Wherever pride had been ripped out by shame, devastation had followed.

His thoughts rushed northward to Haiias's Alaskan Haida. Infamy had touched the Kaigani. They, too, were devastated.

The harbor of Kaigani was too popular with the Iron Men. It was a good place for them to repair a sailing ship, or to get new masts, or to take on wood and water. It was a handy port for them to meet fellow traders, or to pick up a native crew for seal or sea otter hunting. It was also a free and easy haven for wintering seamen. Rum came ashore. Women went shamelessly aboard their vessels.

In Kaigani, horrified Haida eyes watched unbelievable indignities. White sailors guffawed at staggering natives. They made jokes about dead Indians. Diseased Haida girls killed their diseased babies because no medicine man could drive out the evil spirits of the Iron Man's foul sickness. Angry young sea hunters could not find wives. Ferocious, drunken brawls led to murders.

In Kaigani, Eagle Chief Gannyaa (Haiias) and Raven Chief Gu·uu shook their heads in dismay. Their people, possessed by the evil spirits of the white man's firewater, would not listen to them. Before their despairing eyes, their people were sinking into degradation, like many people along the northwest coast.

"That will not happen to the Sdast'a·aas Eagles!" 7idansuu vowed yet again. "Shame is an evil spirit, working among a people." He glanced unhappily at Skawal.

But Gwaii gang·hling was shaking his arm. "Look! Look!" he squealed. "An Iron Man's canoe is coming!"

———————

On that brisk, sunny August day in 1817, French trader Roquifeuil was thankful that noisy, dirty Kaigani was left behind him, and that he was sailing south to the Queen Charlotte Islands.

Even the look of the coast ahead cheered him as he scanned it through his glass. Instead of stark rock, rain forest, and gouged mountain, this was a gentle land. Drifts of blue lupin brightened sand dunes behind long, clean beaches. Cedar houses rimmed the curved beach at Massett, their weathered planks shining silver in the sun beneath fantastic totem poles. Red, white, blue-green, and black paint enlivened poles and beached canoes. In front of the village, like gigantic butterflies, three sleek canoes with double sails skimmed the sparkling waters of the bay. Children played on the beach. A stately chief and a little boy stood beside a canoe. And, somewhere, piles of glossy pelts waited for Capitaine Roquifeuil.

Chief 7idansuu watched the French ship drop anchor. He watched villagers paddle out to meet her.

Massett was not a Sdast'a·aas village. Town Chief Siigee was of a Raven clan. His house was central and biggest. Since it was not a Sdast'a·aas village, 7idansuu did not presume to participate in the trading.

He contented himself with expressing his approval when

Chief Siigee mentioned to him the sale of only two sea otter skins.

"He has poor cloth," Siigee explained as he moved away.

Chief 7idansuu frowned. He turned, and saw a forlorn figure at the ship's rail. The French trader's shoulders sagged; his head hung disconsolately.

A rush of compassion filled 7idansuu. The Haida never suffered the public humiliation of offering inferior goods for sale. Their canoes were the finest of all the canoes on the coast. Their carved spoons were superior. Their furs were the most sought after. Buyers competed briskly.

The French trader looked unhappy.

The French trader was unhappy. The arrogant savages would not sell him their skins. At least, he consoled himself, they would sell him excellent fish, and fowl that, amazingly, did not also taste like fish. And there was sunshine and a breeze to dry out some wet signal flags. He ordered the flags run up.

7idansuu's eyes brightened as he saw the flags run up. These were a ship's words, he knew. "An invitation!" he said happily to his nephew. It was beneath his dignity to go visiting without an invitation; yet he had an overwhelming impulse to honor the trader with a visit that would lift his humiliation. "It's not good for men to be shamed, not even Iron Men," he explained to Gwaii gang·hling. Courtesy was a part of pride. You demanded the best; but you also offered the best, even the best of yourself. "I'll take you boys with me," he said.

He dressed carefully for the visit. In subtle flattery to the Iron Man, he donned a European suit, though without shoes. Over it he put a white woolen blanket-cloak, handsomely bordered with a blue-green Frog pattern. He wore a canoe hat ornamented with his favorite crest, an Eagle, worked out in squared oval abstracts and painted in encircling profiles, in blue-green and black. Then, to complete his elegance, he made a meticulous red zigzag up his nose and up his forehead.

Standing in state in his seventy-two-foot canoe, he was taken out to the ship by an escort of twelve canoes. Skawal stood beside him, every inch an aristocratic Raven in black sea otter. Gwaii gang·hling bobbed around them, comfortably naked except for his breechclout and his canoe hat.

Noting the magnificence, Capitaine Roquifeuil greeted the chief with Old World courtesy. By deferential gestures, he invited him aboard.

Chief 7idansuu acknowledged the invitation as gracefully. Yet he demanded that an Iron Man stay in the canoe as hostage while he himself was on board. Even the friendliest non-Haida stranger was not to be completely trusted.

Still hopeful of trade, the French captain willingly sent his first officer to the canoe. And he continued grandly cordial.

But 7idansuu's observant eyes detected his disappointment. The Iron Man had expected trading, not a social visit. Now he must accept the fact that his trade goods were indeed too poor to sell. How humiliating for him! On generous impulse, he decided to make this courteous man an honorary Haida noble. There was a precedent for it.

Once, a Sdast'a·aas uncle and a great King George man, Captain Douglas, had honored one another by a ceremonial exchange of names. The King George name was still cherished among the Sdast'a·aas, like a crest or song or story. And no doubt the Haida name was as treasured among the members of the King George family. A great name was a great gift. So now, through the ship's interpreter, he made the offer of his name to Capitaine Roquifeuil.

Also through the interpreter, the French captain expressed his gratification at being given an honorary Haida title; and he offered his name in return. "Roquifeuil."

"Lok . . ." Chief 7idansuu shook his head. There was no R

sound in the Haida language, and he began to laugh merrily at his own attempts to pronounce his new French name. His merriment was infectious. The French captain chortled politely. The boys went into gales of laughter.

"Just call it Roki," the trader affably suggested, still not quite appreciating the precise difficulty to a Haida tongue.

The Haida chief proclaimed it proudly. "Loki!" Then he very solemnly pronounced the three august names he was now entitled to wear. "7idansuu! Captain Douglas! Loki!"

Smothering his smiles, the trader struggled as valiantly with his Haida name.

"Itemchou," he finally spelled it that evening in his ship's log. And he added an observation. "This man has a feeling heart." Next day, after a visit ashore, he wrote: "These are the finest men on the northwest coast. They seem better fed, stronger, and much cleaner than the others. In their persons, and in everything belonging to them, there is an appearance of opulence."

"I wonder why," he mused, the day after that, as he sailed away from Massett. Perhaps it was the isolation. He bowed with formal courtesy and true respect to a splendid figure on the beach. Chief 7idansuu had visited him once again; and the second time he had not demanded a hostage. He had displayed utter trust. Too, with one quiet word of command, he had dispersed scores of canoes that were impeding the ship's attempts to free herself after she had run aground. "A real chief," he muttered now. "A remarkable man for a savage!"

Still, it never occurred to Capitaine Roquifeuil that the "savage" had seen him as a humiliated man in need of some royal favor, in need of moral support. Like Skawal.

Year after year after year, the villages along the north coast of Haida Gwaii continued to wear that "appearance of opulence."

As soon as each winter's feasting was over and the bears were emerging from the woods, young men paddled to the west coast to hunt sea lion. When the geese went north, and the silver hordes of tiny eulachon moved into the mainland rivers—pursued by a ravenous army of seals, porpoises, sea lions, killer whales, seagulls, and white-headed eagles—the Haida readied their year's canoes for the annual trip to the mainland. There, canoes and hand-manufactured goods were traded for Nisga'a eulachon oil, Tlingit baskets and copper and Chilkat blankets, and Tsimshian mountain goat horns and tallow.

Before and after the trading, families scattered to halibut and spring salmon fishing stations, or to sea hunting stations. Some went to the head of Massett Inlet, where cedars grew tall and straight for canoes and totem poles. Others went to certain beaches where women and children dug and smoked clams until the first wild rose of summer warned them that the clam season was over and the berry season beginning.

After the berries came the Salmon Moon, and the Cedar Bark Moon. Bears went back into their dens. People went back into their feasthouses for the brief, mild, almost snowless winter. Fires leapt towards the smoke holes. Great houses swirled with color and rang with chants and drumbeats, and filled with the scents of cooking.

The Haida year, like Haida decoration, did not tolerate blank spaces. Both time and space must be filled. Everything had to be squeezed in, but handsomely squeezed in!

Year after year after year, Gwaii gang·hling went visiting with his uncle.

And Skawal, still living at Hiellen, pretended not to care that he was not going off like other Raven princes to take his proper place in the lodge of an honored uncle. He trained diligently for sea hunting, and he excelled in all the boys' games. He seemed not to notice that he lacked the usual devoted attendants, or that he received no new crest to mark his personal belongings.

"We must do something for him," Chief 7idansuu continued to suggest. He consulted respectfully with the boy's Raven relatives, though the subject was very touchy. It was rife with humiliations.

"We could raise his standing with gifts," he proposed. "We could even build a house for him here at Hiellen, and secure fishing stations abandoned by families who have migrated northward." It would require much arranging, he admitted; but it could be arranged. "It's not good for a young man to be humiliated," he reminded people. And he finally managed to start the negotiations.

Skawal shrugged when his mother told him. "I care nothing for the old-fashioned ideas," he declared, flushing hotly.

"I have a great venture in mind," he confided one day to Gwaii gang·hling. He planned to join a Massett group, he said, a group who went to Kaigani every year to be taken, with their dugouts, on board a big hunting schooner. "I'll probably go to California," he boasted to his admiring cousin. "Even to the faraway island where black people swim like dolphins. I'll be greater and richer than any of you here. So I care nothing for your old order." His voice cracked on the claim. His eyes glistened with angry tears.

His young cousin moved closer to him. "You'll be greater and richer than any of us," he fiercely assured Skawal.

Gwaii gang·hling could not help thinking about Skawal when he himself went to a lonely beach to fast and pray and seek for power from a guardian spirit.

He had not eaten for four days when the power came to him in a vision. He had drunk devil's club juice and sea water until he knew he must be as clean and transparent as a crust of ice to any hovering spirit. He was faint with hunger, and asleep, when the vision came.

"It was Master Carpenter himself who came to me," he reported reverently to his uncle, later. Master Carpenter was the supernatural being who could build a feasthouse in one night and still carve his figures so lifelike that they winked at you from his house posts. "And Master Hopper was with him." Master Hopper, as every Haida knew, was the supernatural half-man with one leg, one arm, one eye and ear who always traveled with Master Carpenter. "I saw them both in my vision."

"Master Carpenter himself!" the chief said in awe. "Then you will build great houses and superb canoes. You will carve magnificent totem poles." He made the prediction with absolute conviction.

And Gwaii gang·hling accepted his fate as simply and as completely. "I saw one of the houses," he said, concentrating to recapture that fleeting vision. "It was a house without the crest pole."

His uncle betrayed his concern. "Without a pole?"

"Oh no! It had three poles, but they weren't carved with the owner's crests. They were carved to . . . to tell a story," the imaginative boy went on, trying to see clearly a house that had been only vague and fleeting.

"Story poles." The chief frowned, considering such an innovation. "A myth house . . . Still," he added, with proper deference to the supernatural, "if it came from Master Carpenter, who receives his power directly from the Power-of-the-Shining-Heavens! . . . You say you had been thinking of Skawal?"

Suddenly, the chief's eyes shone with joy. He spoke with glad conviction. "Of course! This is the answer. We'll build Myth House right here. For Skawal! Of course! Of course! Don't you see? Instead of displaying crests that brand Skawal as the nephew of Koyah, his house poles will proclaim the wisdoms of all the generations of all the Haida." These wisdoms, as they both knew, were woven into Haida stories.

"Yes! . . . Yes, Uncle!" Gwaii gang·hling was wild to start the building.

Man and boy, in fact, became obsessed with Myth House. Still, they decided not to divulge the startling innovation until things had been readied for it. Then, at the house-raising potlatch, Gwaii gang·hling would tell of his amazing vision; and Chief 7idansuu himself would tell the stories Myth House illustrated. The whole world would talk about it! Skawal would be widely honored.

"What's his favorite story?" Chief 7idansuu asked his nephew. "We'll carve it on the portal pole."

Gwaii gang·hling, in turn, asked Skawal.

"My favorite story?" Skawal's dark eyes looked as fierce as his Killer Whale crest. "The Mother-in-Law Who Died of Shame," he answered.

A prince was to marry one of the leading princesses of Kwaiskun; but her mother scorned him. She made shameful remarks about him. And the young man, furious and humiliated, wreaked a terrible vengeance on her. First, by using a cedar tree trap, baited with two children, he captured a sea monster. He skinned the sea monster. And then, wearing the supernatural skin, he captured a wealth of sea creatures, one after another, and laid them before his mother-in-law's house, until the woman began to believe she had supernatural power. She became boastful. And when the humiliated youth finally brought a whale to her beach, and when she boastingly claimed that she had captured it with her supernatural powers, the prince revealed the truth. And the woman, overwhelmed by ridicule, died of shame on the beach.

"That is his favorite story," Gwaii gang·hling reported to his uncle.

"And perhaps it's a wise choice for the portal pole of Myth

House," 7idansuu decided. "It will remind people of how dangerous it is to ridicule anybody. Now . . . how shall we illustrate it?"

───────

They were still discussing their symbolic carvings for Myth House, and still choosing their cedars, when Skawal went to Kaigani with the Massett group. He was off on his great adventure!

"You just wait till I get back!" he said to Gwaii gang·hling, squeezing his shoulder. Skawal was now twenty-two; Gwaii gang·hling was seventeen.

"And you just wait till you get back!" his cousin responded mysteriously.

Not long after this, Gwaii gang·hling went to Massett with his uncle. He was on the beach there when a Kaigani canoe grated on the shingle. Anxious-faced paddlers leapt out. They rushed straight to Town Chief Siigee.

"What's happened?" asked Gwaii gang·hling.

He soon heard what had happened.

The Massett group of sea hunters had shipped with a hot-tempered captain, who had had his wife on board the schooner. Both had treated the Haida with cold contempt. The wife, especially, had been disdainful of the Haida.

Stung by this treatment, Skawal in particular had met arrogance with arrogance.

"You insolent savage!" the captain had yelled at him one day. "Put him in irons!" he had ordered. And, to teach all the "savages" a lesson, he had had Skawal flogged on deck.

"Such an insult was not to be borne!" burst out Gwaii gang·hling, hearing about it at Massett.

It had not been borne, his informant told him. Skawal had shot the captain.

"Shot the captain!"

Skawal had shot the captain. He had wounded the captain's wife. Then he had led a native mutiny on the schooner. He had forced the first mate to take the Haida back to Kaigani.

"And then?" Skawal's cousin asked.

The messengers did not know what else had happened. They had been dispatched promptly to Massett to inform the men's relatives of the trouble.

"I'll go at once to Kaigani," Chief 7idansuu offered. "Any relatives can go with me."

"Perhaps we can make reparations to the Boston men," he said anxiously to his nephew. "Perhaps they'll let us atone for the captain's death with sea otter skins." He did not want revenge and killings.

This was the spring of 1829.

A sudden squall delayed their departure for Kaigani. It was a fierce squall that snatched spray from giant waves and set the whole sea smoking. No Haida would cross fifty miles of treacherous ocean while the storm spirits were that angry!

They had to wait till the next morning. Then the canoes rushed northward.

"You are too late, Yatz," Chief Gannyaa (Haiias) said unhappily to his old comrade.

"You're too late, 7idansuu," Chief Gu·uu agreed. "The Massett mutineers went to a firewater feast. Their eyes were not clear when they pushed off for home."

"Yesterday!" said Chief Gannyaa, grimly.

"Pushed off for home yesterday?" 7idansuu was truly aghast. "Skawal ventured out on the sea when that storm was brewing?" Skawal! A highly trained, observant seaman!

"He was not himself," Gu·uu reminded 7idansuu. "He was possessed by the evil spirits of the firewater. Fiercely possessed! No one could stop him. No one!"

Skawal was dead. His humiliations were over. And his cousin wept in secret. "He was going to be so great and rich when he got back," he said sadly to his uncle.

Chief 7idansuu had no time to weep. His concern, now, was the welfare of the living.

The Boston schooner had fled. He could do nothing to forestall the expected revenge.

He could, however, do something to compensate families of the men Skawal had led to their deaths. He could personally make restitution to them; Skawal's own Raven relatives were unlikely to do it. "And I will not have him shamed any further," he told his nephew. Skawal had not been his, a Sdast'a·aas Saang gaahl Eagle, but he had been dear to his father's brother.

He was restless to get back home. Kaigani was most depressing. The degradation appalled him.

"Before you go," Gu·uu implored 7idansuu, "come and hear the words of an Iron Man who is not a fur trader. I think he's a sorcerer." Gu·uu scowled before he went on. "7idansuu, I want to know what you think of Mr. Green."

Gwaii gang·hling accompanied the chiefs to the Reverend Mr. Green's barque, *Volunteer*. And the Haida youth could see that Mr. Green was indeed a sorcerer. He held a charm that he called *The Book*. It was a packet of ghost leaves. And before he could gaze at *The Book*, Mr. Green put twin circles of the-ice-that-does-not-melt before his eyes. *The Book*, an interpreter said, revealed that men must not steal, nor kill, nor drink rum.

"Then why did the Iron Men bring rum?" 7idansuu demanded to know. "Why did they change the good way we lived?" In the old days, he claimed, people did not steal and kill and drink the poisoned water that drove skillful young seamen out onto the ocean while the storm spirits were angry. "Why did they bring rum?" he challenged.

Because *money* was the root of all evil, the interpreter explained to the Haida.

Money?

Money was strings of dentalium shells.

Dentalium shells were evil? Gwaii gang·hling found it most confusing.

"God is not the Power-of-the-Shining-Heavens," commented Chief Gu·uu, who had talked before with the missionary. "He is the Old-Man-of-the-Sky, an old man with a beard, 7idansuu."

"And God does not like heathen idols," the Reverend Mr. Green told them. *The Book* revealed that people should not make a graven image. The totem pole was a graven image. And a graven image was heathen and wicked. People with a graven image would be thrown into a burning lake, he assured them. People with totem poles would be hurled into the lake to burn forever.

The Haida were astounded. They consulted one another with anxious faces. If 7idansuu had no totem pole, they argued, how could people know he was descended from Copper Woman? How would Eagle strangers know they could find brothers in this lodge? How could Raven visitors know that here they could find husbands for their nieces? How could the young people remember their family's history if there were no crests to remind them of the important events in the lives of their ancestors? If you could not carve a Killer Whale or an Eagle or a Frog or a Bear, how could anybody tell whose canoe was whose canoe; whose fish club was whose fish club; whose house was whose house? How could a society manage without identifying crests? How could a graven image be wicked?

The potlatch was evil, also, Mr. Green assured the Haida. And the dancing was evil also.

The chiefs raised surprised eyebrows again. They consulted

again, together. How could these things be evil when they were the very things the Power-of-the-Shining-Heavens had given them to live by? Even as God had given white men *The Book!* How could you possibly manage life without the public witnessing of claims at a potlatch? And without paying the witnesses for their service? And without first reassuring those witnesses by having the chiefs dance the dance of welcome and scatter the eagle-down of peace and friendship? How could you gain the spirit power you needed if you couldn't honor supernatural beings with a ritual dance? How could you ensure the harvest of the waters if you did not dance reverently to honor the Chief of the Salmon People when he arrived? How could you live spiritually?

Gwaii gang·hling found it all more and more confusing.

A particular thing troubled Gu·uu. He could understand God. He could understand prayer; prayer was part of his own life. But, he wanted to know, why did the Iron Men pray without reverence? He had heard them, many times, calling on God. But they didn't do it with the trembling respect of the native supplicator. They called angrily, and they usually added the word "Damn!" What did it mean?

"It means that Iron Men are often wicked," the Reverend Mr. Green said, wiping his forehead with his big bandana.

Chief 7idansuu invited him to come to Hiellen to talk more about these things, but Mr. Green had other commitments. So the chief and his nephew went back to Haida Gwaii confused, as well as unhappy over Skawal.

But the salmon came and the roses bloomed and the berries ripened and the mild, brief winter came to the islands, as these things had always come. And the feasthouses began to warm again with blazing fires, and songs, and laughter.

F I V E

IT WAS IN THE MIDDLE OF THE WINTER that a strange message came from Tanu, a message that recalled again the words of Mr. Green.

Tanu was an east coast village with a famous medicine man, Kwanduhadgaa.

Kwanduhadgaa had achieved marvelous cures with herbs and charms, rattle and incantations. Now, like lesser men, he was defeated by the new sicknesses that had come with the Iron Men.

But he did not accept defeat. He merely needed another power, he said, to combat these new evil spirits. And being dedicated to his own fame as well as to his people's health, he prepared himself to acquire this power.

He cleansed himself ceremonially with devil's club juice and with sea water. He fasted until he seemed to be a cadaver, until his long, uncombed, unwashed hair straggled over scarred, ghastly emaciation. Then he laid aside his crown of carved horn tips, and the carved bone charms that no longer served him.

He would go into a deep trance, he announced. His soul would leave his body and climb up the long Sky Ladder. And there, above, he would gain the new power to drive out the new evil spirits.

Before he lay down, he instructed the Tanu people. He showed them a long strip of cedar bark treated to burn very slowly, and marked into sections by bands of paint.

"Between these strips is one hour," he told them.

"*Hour*?" They repeated the strange word, and wondered.

When the bark had burned through four hours, they were to wake him, he said. By that time his soul would have returned to his body, and he would know what it was the people must do to be rid of the new pestilences.

The people agreed solemnly.

The spirit self of Kwanduhadgaa left his body and climbed up the long Sky Ladder (he told them later). He came to a village surrounded by a wall, and there was a gate, through which he must enter. The gate of silvered cedar was so richly inlaid with abalone mother-of-pearl that it glistened with iridescent rainbows, like a leaping salmon. And guarding this shining gate was a man with a gigantic musket. The man was black; his hands were grown to the musket.

This black man looked at him and sniffed, as if he smelled a rotting carcass. Then he spoke angrily. "Look down at the villages!"

Kwanduhadgaa glanced down.

But where were the villages?

The inland wilderness of mountain and forest had crept to

the very shores of Haida Gwaii. Everywhere waves lapped at empty beaches.

Alarmed, his spirit self flew right around the Haida islands. But where were the villages? There were no houses at Tanu. No totem poles. Nor at Skedans, or Cumshewa.

Moving north along the east coast, he came to Skidegate. Here there were poles and houses. Here there were canoes. Here there were people moving, but the people did not seem happy.

His spirit self flew on, northward, more and more aghast at the aching silence. There was nothing even at Tlell, nothing but the long, lonely, lovely beaches. There was nothing at Nii-kun, the long nose jutting through the ocean. He rounded the spit and flew west. There was nothing at Hiellen . . . Yaakun . . . Skou-an. Only silent stretches of hard-packed sand.

There was a town at Massett! But none at Yaan . . . Tlaas kwun . . . Yeltatzie. Nothing at K'yuusdaa . . . Dadens.

Trembling with dread, he flew south along the west coast of the islands. Here the wild sea hurled itself angrily against the rocks and reefs; but nobody saw it. Nobody heard its fury. Only seagulls screamed and ravens cried out and eagles circled high above them. Only the dorsal fins of killer whales sliced through the lonely ocean.

"What has happened to the villages?" he implored the black man whose hands were grown to the musket.

"God has wiped them out because He does not like two things: the heathen totem poles of the Haida, and the smell of the corpses in the mortuary poles."

"God?"

"The Old-Man-with-the-Beard," the black man explained, "as mighty as the Power-of-the-Shining-Heavens." He opened the gate to show him.

But Kwanduhadgaa could not see God, at first. He saw only a burning lake. People screamed in the flames; screamed to die in the burning lake, but they could not die. "God is punishing them for the totem poles and for the smell of the grave boxes in the mortuary poles," the black man told Kwanduhadgaa. Then he took him along to see God.

But God was so shining that Kwanduhadgaa could not look at him.

Then the people woke him up, and he found himself back in Tanu.

He told them what he had seen.

"Tanu wiped out?" they gasped in fear.

"All the villages wiped out!" His eyes burned with uncanny fire. "All except Massett and Skidegate."

The thought was staggering to the Tanu people. Yet they could well believe this warning vision. Once, their own legends told them, there had been a flood. It, too, had wiped out the villages. It, too, had left few survivors. It, too, had come as a punishment because of bad things the people were doing.

"The villages wiped out," they kept repeating.

"Except Massett and Skidegate."

"And a lake of fire where people screamed but could not die!"

"God was punishing them for their totem poles, and for their corpses in the mortuary totem poles."

"But . . ."

It was unthinkable that totem poles could be bad.

Still, Kwanduhadgaa was a famous man. And his soul had climbed the Sky Ladder just to find out what must be done to drive out the new evil spirits. Perhaps only the white man's God had the power to combat the white man's sicknesses. Perhaps the Haida people would have to—

But it was unthinkable!

Word of Kwanduhadgaa's warning vision rushed around the Haida islands in that winter of 1829–30. In every feasthouse it was told, retold, and discussed in awful whispers.

God did not like the totem poles.

At Hiellen, a group of people danced reverently to placate this new dreaded power.

"But God does not like dancing, either," Chief 7idansuu said to the people.

In Eagle House, they could not forget Kwanduhadgaa's vision even when the flames leapt towards the smoke hole and the drums beat and the people chanted; even when the storytellers told them the best-loved legends; even when young men whipped soapberries up into a luscious pink froth and people sucked in its bittersweetness. The tiny paddles they ate with were painted with crests; their handles were carved with crests. Maybe even a berry paddle was a graven image. Maybe even berry paddles were evil.

One young visitor did not seem to be as desolated as all the others. This was Skil ta qa dju, the heir of Town Chief Siigee of Massett. "Massett will survive," he noted with satisfaction. And his eyes glittered. With a new ambition?

Skil ta qa dju, an Eagle prince, was already a young man of some importance. To him, signs of change were as exhilarating as the brisk winds that cleared off a sea fog.

Gwaii gang·hling found Skil ta qa dju curiously interested in Myth House.

"We'll still build Myth House," 7idansuu had decided after Skawal's death. "After all, the vision came from Master Carpenter," he pointed out to his nephew, "and we can't afford to offend him. Besides, Eagle House is growing old. These posts won't stand forever."

"You would live in Myth House?" Gwaii gang·hling had been truly astounded. "You would live in a house that doesn't display the Sdast'a·aas crests and the Saang gaahl crests on the portal pole?"

"I've been thinking," his uncle answered. "Now, with the iron tools, it's simpler to carve totem poles. So why couldn't we display our crests on the detached poles, and carve other things on our house poles? The more I think about a house with story poles, the better I like it. So! Let's build Myth House for ourselves! And let's tell the people our plans now. After all, their chief's house is their house."

The people had been startled when he told them about it. They had argued freely and loudly about such an innovation; but in the end they had decided for it. Sdast'a·aas Eagles—and especially Sdast'a·aas Saang gaahl Eagles—had the prestige needed to launch a new style, they reminded one another with considerable gratification. They would even gain glory from it. They began to be thrilled about Myth House.

That was before the word came from Tanu.

Now, Kwanduhadgaa's vision raised a dank, uncomfortable fog around every kind of totem pole, even a story pole for a new house.

Gwaii gang·hling noticed, however, that Skil ta qa dju did not lose his interest in Myth House. "He's too interested in it," he protested to his uncle.

The chief shook his head in mild reproof. "No Eagle can be too interested in another Eagle clan's feasthouse."

Biggest! That word started a train of thought in Gwaii gang·hling's head. Skil ta qa dju had quizzed him especially about the size of Myth House. "He mentioned that they need a new house at Massett. Perhaps Chief Siigee—"

His uncle waived even a suggestion of unseemly ambition. "All men are ambitious," he reminded Gwaii gang·hling.

"Well," his nephew conceded. But Skil ta qa dju *is* ambitious, he thought.

As if reading his mind, the chief smiled and said, "It's good for young men to be full of pride in themselves."

And they both thought of Skawal, who had not been allowed to have enough pride in himself.

"I wish he could have lived in Myth House," Gwaii gang·hling said softly.

Somehow, they could not get started on Myth House, and it wasn't altogether reluctance caused by Kwanduhadgaa's vision. The project had to be postponed, and postponed.

Muskets had so depleted the sea otter herds that the marine fur trade was no longer an important source of wealth. Of necessity, emphasis had turned back to the canoe trade, the traditional source of Haida wealth and prestige.

That year of 1830, and the next year and the next year, the best cedars were needed for canoes; the best woodcutters were chipping at dugouts; the head chief was visiting canoe-making camps.

Every Haida canoe must be perfect, he reminded Eagle canoe-makers. One inferior canoe could degrade all Haida canoes. The nation's wealth and prestige rested on the absolute perfection of its famous product.

"I have never heard of a canoe that was a failure," one white man observed. "They run it out on the water and there, like a bird, it floats, a thing of beauty without a flaw!"

Gwaii gang·hling decorated, with growing skill and excitement. He learned how to achieve a tenseness of feeling and a beauty of design. He discovered how to repeat the line of his flattened oval in the leading edge of a bird's wing, or on an identifying whale fin.

Haida wealth also rested on slave-trading; and slave-trading had to be preceded by slave-raiding, an occupation that had become infinitely more hazardous since the advent of the white man.

The three lordly northern native linguistic groups, Haida,

Tlingit, and Tsimshian, had always provided their chiefs with slaves. They had always found these slaves along the coast to the south. And it was often the Haida who snatched them.

There had always been fierce nations along that coast to the south; these nations had always resisted capture of their people by the sea dogs from Haida Gwaii. But now they had muskets! At long last, they could wreak vengeance on the arrogant Haida. They waited like angry wasps. They darted out armed with muskets, and with centuries of bitter hatred.

That summer of 1830, both of Gwaii gang·hling's older brothers were ambushed along the coast. Both were killed.

And so, with startling suddenness, at eighteen, Gwaii gang·hling was heir to the hereditary head chieftainship of the proud Sdast'a·aas Eagles. He was married to a Raven princess. The enormity of the change overwhelmed him. "How can I hope to be a great chief?" he implored his uncle. "I haven't even proved myself as a warrior yet."

"Perhaps the warrior's day is passing," his uncle consoled him. "Still, we do need slaves. And any chief must have the respect of his warriors, too."

To win this respect, Gwaii gang·hling went on the slave raids.

"This is where you belong, Chief!" one of the warriors told him; and the man's eyes were frankly admiring the youth's tall, handsome figure, and his commanding presence.

His prince did not agree; but he could not shirk his duty. The Haida did need slaves, he agreed, to free them for artistic pursuits. But he sighed very deeply. From now on he, like his uncle, must regard carving and painting and copper-smithing as his lesser occupations.

Still, there was one compensation. Now he was out on the sea more, and Gwaii gang·hling loved the ocean. He had always gloried in it. He was a born sea captain.

He did not abandon Myth House. He merely postponed it for the time being. Sitting by a campfire, he often considered the three story poles that would ornament its face. The taller, central pole would illustrate "The Mother-in-Law Who Died of Shame." But what of the two matching corner poles? He talked to many storytellers, and storytelling was a great profession. Each one seemed to have yet another adventure to tell of Yaahl (Raven), and the tales were frequently contradictory.

"Raven's beginning to possess me," he laughingly confessed to his uncle. "He makes me choose among the variations, and then tie them all together into one epic."

"Then we'll have Raven for our corner house poles," Chief 7idansuu decided. His face wrinkled with amusement. Raven was a lively prankster. His adventures often sent the feasthouse into gales of laughter. "Which tale shall we illustrate on Myth House?"

"That's what's so hard to decide," Gwaii gang·hling told him. "There are so many adventures!" He stood lost in thought for the next few minutes. "Raven is very, very funny," he said. "But Uncle, Raven is very sad, too."

"I leave the choice to you."

"When we raise the house," the younger man suggested, "perhaps I can tell Raven's whole long story at the potlatch. I'm not a storyteller; but I think so much about it, trying to weave all the scattered bits together, that I think I can do it."

"You'll tell it," the chief assured him. "And you'll tell it superbly, for you have a feeling heart."

Yaahl (Raven) the Wonder Worker had been involved in Creation. He had brought the first people out of a primeval clamshell on the beach at the northeastern tip of Haida Gwaii. It was only after the Flood that he became Yaahl the Trickster.

After the Flood, Yaahl dropped from the Sky and landed on a tangle of floating kelp. As a radiant spirit child, he was rescued and adopted by a chief and chieftainess who had just lost their own dear son. He was given a cloak of white feathers.

Being supernatural, Yaahl could fly in the feather blanket, disguised as a giant bird.

A spirit child did not need human food, and he had been cautioned in the Sky not to eat it. But his human relatives were concerned for his health; and at last he was tempted and tricked into eating.

The wrath of the Sky fell on him. He was possessed by the evil spirits of gluttony. His entire energies were directed towards satisfying his endless appetite. He played fantastic pranks on people and animals to get their food for himself. Once, escaping from a feasthouse in his white bird disguise, Yaahl stuck fast in the smoke hole; and his feathers turned black.

Finally, after many awful and hilarious adventures, Yaahl, desperate with shame for his own gluttony, banished himself to the mountains.

Gathering these adventures, and weaving them into one epic tale, Gwaii gang·hling found himself laughing and weeping by turn. Raven was so very funny, and yet so tragic. But which of the marvelous adventures should be illustrated on the corner poles of Myth House? One day he enlisted his own little heir, Da·a̱xiigang, in the decision.

Da·a̱xiigang, a sister's son, lived in the east coast village of Skidegate. He was a pale, sickly child.

"Which Raven tale do you like best?" Gwaii gang·hling asked him; and he tried not to let his eyes betray his concern over the thin, bony rib cage. "Don't decide now! Take lots of time to think about it!"

The Iron Man's sicknesses that had driven Kwanduhadgaa up the long Sky Ladder were now threatening the Sdast'a·aas chiefly line. In Skidegate, death kept striking the lodge where Gwaii gang·hling's sister was trying to raise his heirs. Child after child died. Now there was only Da·axiigang, and his frail body was wracked by coughs.

"Give him lots of eulachon grease," the young man repeatedly implored his sister. "And seaweed." They both knew how strengthening these particular foods were.

One day during that same visit to Skidegate, Gwaii gang·hling chanced on little Da·axiigang when the boy was whittling a piece of cedar. At least, his uncle had thought it was merely whittling. But he caught his breath at the salmon he saw emerging from the wood. He laid a fond hand on the skinny shoulder.

Da·axiigang looked up. "Uncle," he asked eagerly, "where do the salmon go?"

"To their winter village out at sea, where they take on their human form," Gwaii gang·hling informed his heir. And to prove the truth of this statement, he told him the story of "The Prince Who Was Taken Away by the Salmon."

Da·axiigang listened, wide eyed, and occasionally open mouthed, too. Then he resumed his carving while he thought about it.

He was such a winsome, eager little boy, his uncle thought. And he would not live long.

All the relatives feared that. All tried to nourish him and protect him. Women gave him the choicest bits of crab and the plumpest berries. Men nodded approval when he was not made to stand in the icy sea with the other young boys, to make them tougher, and when he was not taken offshore with the other children to capsize a canoe and learn to right it in deep, frigid water.

Gwaii gang·hling's heart sank lower at every visit. Yet he concealed his fears from his nephew.

"Uncle, why do we scatter eagle-down as a token of peace?" Da·axiigang asked him one day, a few years later.

"Because of the Flood," the young man explained. And he told how the angry waters had risen and risen until even the highest mountain peaks were about to be submerged. Then eagles and seagulls and even swans had started shaking feathers down on the heaving waters. And the waters had stilled; they had receded like an ebb tide. So the surviving people had realized that white feathers were the sign of peace.

"Like an ebb tide," the child said, picking up his uncle's phrase. "Uncle, why does the tide ebb and flow?"

Gwaii gang·hling explained that it was because of the Old-Woman-with-the-Tide-Lines.

His heir listened with lively interest. Then, suddenly remembering something else, he unwrapped an oiled skin from a treasure he had been saving to give his uncle.

"A salmon!" Gwaii gang·hling started at the beauty of it. Da·axiigang had carved it from the recently discovered slate, mined on a mountain near Skidegate. The carving was crude, but the slate had been rubbed until it was as glossy black as the wing of a raven. "My heart feels good!" he said, scrutinizing the childish carving with true delight.

"But I wish it were of some use," the boy told his uncle apologetically. He knew that carving should be done to make useful things beautiful. A slate salmon was completely useless.

The slate, called argillite, carved as easily as a piece of wood. Polished, it glittered like a raven's eye. But it was too heavy for a fish club, too fragile to be a hammer.

Wood, whalebone, horn: these things were good to carve,

Da·axiigang knew. They were useful. Slate was not useful. But it was so beautiful when it was carved and polished! Even old, old carvers could not resist its beauty. They carved useless, intricate things from slate and then called them Iron Men's pipes, though no Iron Man could ever smoke them. Old eyes shone, as the wrinkled fingers of the old men caressed these exquisite nothings.

"I wish it were of some use," Da·axiigang repeated wistfully to his uncle.

"It is of some use," his uncle assured him. "This salmon makes my heart feel good, Da·axiigang."

It also made his heart feel bad, for it showed how gifted his sickly heir was; and he would not grow up. He would never preside at Myth House. "Have you decided which Raven story for the corner poles?" he asked very gently.

"Raven and the Halibut Fisherman," the boy announced. "Uncle! If we could only make Raven in slate!"

His uncle tousled his hair. "Make Raven in slate for me."

"Oh, I will. I will! . . . But . . . I wish it were some use, Uncle."

"It's of much use, Da·axiigang. It gives skill to your eyes and fingers." But this lad would not need skill. He would never live to decorate a superb canoe. He would never grow up to make his claim, either, to the head chieftainship of the Sdast'a·aas Eagles.

Maybe the Eagle head chieftainship would pass to another family. Perhaps the Saang gaahl line of chiefs was doomed to be wiped out.

He shook off Kwanduhadgaa's vision.

As time went by, however, it was harder and harder to dismiss the ambitions of Town Chief Siigee of Massett and his heir, Skil ta qa dju.

They were preparing timbers for a new house at Massett. Rumor said it was going to be the biggest house on the north coast of Haida Gwaii. The biggest on any coast! And it would have a story pole, too. A startling story pole! No one knew what it might be.

"They couldn't build a house bigger than yours," Gwaii gang·hling protested to his uncle one day.

"Oh, Siigee wouldn't be the first chief to try to raise his standing," said 7idansuu, his thoughts on Koyah. "Times are changing. Why, even our own heirs—"

"Da·axiigang must live!" his nephew burst out. "The Sdast'a·aas need wisdom now, and not ambition."

Chief Siigee died in the 1840s. Skil ta qa dju became the new town chief of Massett, taking the name 7wii·aa. Chief 7idansuu also died. And as his heir, Gwaii gang·hling led his people to a new home in K'yuusdaa. His uncle's ancient, honored crests were carved on a memorial totem pole that was to stand in front of Myth House.

Myth House was at last ready for raising. Poles and house posts had been carved, wide cedar planks split; timbers had been channeled to receive the wall planks; everybody had been invited to the house-raising potlatch: from Massett, Skidegate, Cumshewa, Kaigani, and a dozen other places. Everyone came.

Everyone exclaimed with admiration when the house was standing. Always architecturally pleasing, the traditional Haida house had reached a new peak of beauty here, they all agreed. Iron tools allowed deeper, more elaborate carving.

Deeper carving made lurking shadows.

Da·axiigang's gaze surged up the poles, and down, and then up again, appreciating superb, startling decoration. The grotesque heads with their identifying symbols were terrifying. He shivered at the central shame pole. The characters seemed to have been frozen at their fiercest moments. If they could just *burst* out, he felt, what might they not do! To one another! To him! It was marvelously horrifying.

Like the house, the potlatch too was more elaborate than in the old days. Dance masks were more numerous and more ingeniously contrived to startle or to amuse with sound and movement. And now there were woolen blankets to give, as well as fur pelts. There were bracelets and anklets of silver and gold, made of melted-down coins, as well as copper.

Gwaii gang·hling had been the one seized with the notion of melting down coins; he himself was a masterly jeweler. And now, before the gifts were distributed, as the new Chief 7idansuu, he made a flamboyant gesture. To dramatize the wealth of the Sdast'a·aas Saang gaahl Eagles, and perhaps to impress Town Chief 7wii·aa, he burned a new canoe in the feast-house. Its flames glinted on many big copper shields engraved with Haida crests. Cheers and chanting and drumbeats almost drowned out the whispers about Kwanduhadgaa.

The new Chief 7idansuu told his Raven epic.

And there were new, exciting events to talk about. A new wave of Boston men had reached Haida waters. These were the New England whalers. Many wintered at Skidegate now. They picked up Haida sea hunters with their equipment, because Haida men had the skill needed to make the stealthy approach on the gigantic sperm whale. And these Haida whalermen had adventures to relate at Myth House.

Too, there was a new, permanent fur-trading post on the mainland, nearby.

Life was exciting, even if haunted by an awful vision.

The new Chief 7idansuu, now in his early thirties, made his claim to the town chieftainship of K'yussdaa. And the Sdast'a·aas Saang gaahl Eagles were wealthy enough to distribute yet more piles of gifts to the witnesses at this second potlatch. They would be wealthier still, they knew, when the gifts were returned in the traditional way, with interest.

Lavish as they were, the K'yuusdaa potlatches were, in some

respects, eclipsed by Massett potlatches.

Town Chief 7wii·aa, too, raised a memorial pole—to Siigee; and the pole was slightly higher than the 7idansuu pole.

Then, as Chief 7wii·aa, he raised his house. It was a bigger house than Myth House. In fact, it was named Big House. And it was ornamented with a story pole that really set the tongues clacking throughout Haida Gwaii.

It was a Ⱪingii pole!

Ⱪingii was the supernatural father of White Raven, the original Yaahl. And Ⱪingii was raising a new totem pole when the Flood struck the world. Many people had gathered for his potlatch.

When the Flood waters began to rise all around them, Ⱪingii's relatives and guests started scrambling up the pole to keep from being drowned.

So White Raven the Wonder Worker lighted on top of the pole, and by his magic he caused it to grow and grow as the waters rose.

The totem pole became a gigantic tree, filled with the survivors of the Flood.

Ⱪingii and his people had survived the past catastrophe.

The pole reminded everybody that Chief 7wii·aa and his Massett people would survive the coming catastrophe.

S I X

AWAY FROM HAIDA GWAII, TOO, the old order was being challenged. Rebellion was stirring among the neighbors as well as within the family.

The Haida had always respected two great neighboring groups: the Tsimshian people living east of them on the mainland, and the Tlingit people to the north in Alaska.

These three northern nations traded in wary friendship. And they were notably similar in social organization, cultural traditions, and totem poles.

There was one difference, though; and it was a difference that tilted the delicate balance of native prestige.

The Haida were sea rovers. The Tsimshian and Tlingit were

masters of the wild rivers that plunged through the coast range, and of the tide rips that raced among the islands fringing the coast. The Haida darted easily over to the mainland, usually to trade, occasionally to raid; but seldom did a Tsimshian or a Tlingit dare to cross the ocean to Haida Gwaii. Practically never did he raid.

The Haida, and only the Haida, were immune from attack.

In consequence, the pride of the Haida shaded even that of their mighty neighbors. They were the lords of the coast, the aristocrats of their world.

But suddenly the Tsimshian began to challenge this supremacy. They had something to balance the scales. In 1831, the year the New England whalers began wintering at Skidegate, the Hudson's Bay Company established a permanent fur-trading post at Place of Roses in Tsimshian territory on the mainland. Eagle Chief Lagaahl, a toweringly important Tsimshian, loaned the Company one of his own camping sites for Fort Simpson. He could not give the Company the land, he explained, because all the land belonged to all the Tsimshian.

This prudent old English fur-trading company insured the safety and prosperity of Fort Simpson even before it raised the log palisades. Chief Trader Kennedy married Eagle Chief Lagaahl's daughter Sudaahl, an important Wolf princess, thereby allying himself with the two most important local factions, and also upsetting the balance of power in the north.

The Haida scowled at news of the marriage. None of their chiefs had a marriage alliance with a mighty Iron chief.

The Tsimshian smiled. Regarding Mr. Kennedy now as their relative, they abandoned nine ancient villages along Metlakatla Pass to settle under the protecting cannons of his fort. Their cedar houses and totem poles soon rimmed the beach west of the palisades. The annual intertribal trading of the Haida, Tsimshian, and Tlingit moved from camps along the Nass River to this new settlement near its mouth.

Chief 7idansuu frowned. Though he was thankful for a steady fur market, and for a reliable source of muskets, ammunition, and excellent Hudson's Bay blankets, he knew there was bad blood between Lagaahl and some of the Haida Eagles. Once, Town Chief Siigee of Massett had made the grave error of capturing Lagaahl's sister Waaniiks during a raid.

True, she had been treated with honor in Haida Gwaii; reparations had been paid; the stain of her captivity had been wiped out at a potlatch; the dance of peace had been danced and much eagle-down blown over both sides. Siigee's heir, the present Chief 7wii·aa, had married a Tsimshian princess to cement good relations. Yet there was bad blood.

Tinder awaited only a spark.

Chief Trader Kennedy was aware of this danger. Still, year after year he thrilled to the arrival of the Haida at Fort Simpson. Succeeding fleets of canoes flew over the sea with white wings. Well offshore, the sails were furled. Then long paddles dipped with rhythmic precision, keeping time to a chant. Towering prows sliced the water.

"Magnificent!" he always murmured. Then he always added, "And no fighting this time, please Heaven!"

The Tsimshian watched the arrival with more calculating eyes. These were the new canoes, brought over for trading. The Haida would go back to their islands in old trade-ins, patched for the return crossing of a hundred miles of formidable ocean. Only the state canoes of the head chiefs would not be for sale.

The Haida always camped east of the palisades. And the Tsimshian, secure at last under the cannons of their relative Mr. Kennedy, were no longer so much in awe of the sea dogs. A Tsimshian would now occasionally dare to tweak the nose of some too arrogant Haida.

One day when the air was fragrant with wild roses and the

salmonberry bushes were dripping with yellow-orange fruit, Chief Lagaahl's daughter-in-law was conducting trade with Taawhlgee, niece of a lesser Sdast'a·aas town chief. They were trading Tsimshian eulachon oil for Haida dried halibut; and Taawhlgee was being exceedingly arrogant.

The annoyed Tsimshian chieftainess spoke sharply to her, accusing her of short measure.

Incensed by the insult, Taawhlgee struck the other across the face with a dried halibut.

The war was on!

For two days men battled, and the entrenched Tsimshian had the advantage at Fort Simpson.

"We'll be clubbed to death like seals on the beach," Haida warriors raged. They always fought on the sea, standing back to back along the center of a canoe.

The Tsimshian, river men, were more accustomed to land warfare. They slaughtered scores of Haida while sustaining few casualties themselves.

Chief Trader Kennedy and Chief Lagaahl and Chief 7idansuu finally managed to bring the combatants to a dance of peace. Reparations were paid to ease the departure of the ghosts of the dead. But the Haida left, smarting under defeat.

The Haida defeated by the Tsimshian! It was unbelievable. They seethed with shame. They darted home like wasps.

In public at Fort Simpson they had supported Taawhlgee to the death. Once they reached the privacy of Haida Gwaii, however, they turned on her to kill her.

Her uncle, the lesser town chief, intervened on her behalf. He impoverished himself making restitution to people who had lost sons and nephews. Then he himself dealt with Taawhlgee. He stripped her of her name, her rank, and her crests. He gave her to a Massett subchief as a slave wife. This, too, would ease the ghosts' departure, since one noble was worth many common people. 7idansuu approved the punishment, for a chieftainess's responsibility was not only the welfare of her people but also the maintenance of Haida dignity abroad.

The whole village was humiliated by what its chieftainess had done. And 7idansuu did what he could to lift their shame. He visited the village and distributed gifts. He further honored and heartened the people by telling them his three-day Raven epic at a feast.

Men as well as women were growing more and more touchy these days, he noted. Futile hostility against contemptuous Iron Men and their cannons vented itself in fury against other native people, just as rapids stopped by a rock wall turn to thunder against a mere boulder. He frowned as anxiously over the future of his Eagles as over the health of Da·axiigang. Both were close to his heart.

A baby was expected at Myth House. This was a very special baby, for the expectant mother was 7idansuu's wife.

"It'll be a girl," the chief whispered hopefully. A girl would be a good omen for Da·axiigang. The birth of a princess would seem to foretell that the ancient pattern was once more destined to be followed, the Haida pattern of the chief's daughter marrying his heir to keep the bloodline strong.

A boy was born at Myth House.

Chief 7idansuu sighed.

Yet soon the child Gu·uu was the delight of his father. He was as round and rosy and lively as 7idansuu wished Da·axiigang could have been. Occasionally he was so lively that his father was tempted to clout him with his exquisitely carved fish club.

––––––––

Once, late in the springtime of 1850, they were all at Fort Simpson with the year's canoes.

Da·aхiigang, who was now a skinny ten-year-old, had come to the mainland with the Skidegate Ravens; for his Raven fathers (his actual father and his father's brothers) were famous canoe-makers from that east coast village.

Chief 7idansuu and his family had arrived with the Sdast'a·aas Eagles after camping on an offshore island.

On that offshore island, one of his hunters had shot such a remarkably fine deer that he presented it to Chief Trader Kennedy.

The chief trader at Fort Simpson was unexpectedly excited about this gift.

"It was shot with a gold bullet," he exclaimed to Chief 7idansuu. "Look! Gold!"

"Sometimes we run out of iron bullets," the Haida calmly explained.

"But . . . gold!" Chief Trader Kennedy showed his gold ring, his watch and chain, and several coins to demonstrate the value of this metal. "Where did it come from?" he asked.

Chief 7idansuu did not know, but he promised to find out. Gold might prove to be another valuable trade item for the Haida.

"And don't tell anyone except me!" Mr. Kennedy implored him. "I'll pay you a blanket for every pipeful of gold your people can bring me." He presented the chief with a number of large tobacco pipes to serve as measures. Then he recalled that Dr. McLoughlin, the "Great White-Headed Eagle" of Fort Vancouver on the Columbia River, had reported a piece of gold quartz from the Queen Charlottes away back in the 1830s. The Company had not followed up the clue. "I'll pay blankets even for rock with gold in it," he told 7idansuu. "But don't show it to other traders!" The Company had no wish to have its fur-trading wilderness invaded by hordes of men—like California, where a gold rush had started the previous year, 1849.

7idansuu asked his hunter where the bullet had come from. The man remembered that he had won it while gambling with Skidegate relatives. His relatives had also acquired it while gambling.

7idansuu decided to initiate the search for gold immediately. He also decided to keep the matter private until the source was located. Only then could ownership of the site be established and trading rules negotiated. This new trade must be launched in a peaceful and orderly manner. It must not become a source of trouble among the Haida themselves.

"Skidegate," he muttered, and he recalled seeing a woman in that village showing a piece of yellow-veined quartz to her friends. So he consulted Da·axiigang, who was from Skidegate.

The boy instantly named the woman. Fortunately she was a Sdast'a·aas Eagle who would be glad to guide her head chief. He was almost sure she had found the gold quartz on the west coast of Haida Gwaii, south of Skidegate Channel. And he begged to be taken along.

"Well . . . 7idansuu hesitated. But the boy's face was so eager. "Yes!" he decided, with a burst of enthusiasm for the venture. "We'll make this a family camping trip. We'll take Gu·uu and his mother, with just a couple of slaves to paddle a small canoe."

———

As this canoe moved off from Skidegate a month later, sunlight yellowed seaweed that clung to rocks. Ravens combed the breeze with wide, fingered wings. And eagles swooped from crags, sending little oyster-catchers scooting over the water so fast that their black-and-white wings twinkled.

Captaining the canoe himself, 7idansuu steered happily past timbered islets and into Skidegate Channel. He had grown up in these waters. As Gwaii gang·hling, he had learned to master the treacherous passage from ocean to ocean.

Skidegate Channel cuts Haida Gwaii in two. Eight miles long, it is so narrow that, for one stretch, trees almost meet above it. And since the tides are considerably higher on the confined eastern end than on the open west, the turn of the tide does not produce the customary reversible falls. The sea races through the gorge in such an unusual way that the crossing can be attempted only at high water, and then only by expert seamen.

Da·axiigang found it exhilarating. Though delicate and protected, he had Haida blood; and that blood surged now with the sea daring of his race.

Little Gu·uu clapped his hands with delight at the porpoises that rushed through the gorge with them, leaping almost into the boat and thrashing their tails wildly near it. Then, as they neared the western end of the channel, he began to cling to his mother. His eyes widened with alarm.

The roar of the open Pacific had begun to pound at them, and it was as if they were racing straight into the open jaws of a sea monster.

"It's Kagwaii!" Da·axiigang shouted in mock terror. And he gave himself up to the delicious horror of envisioning the legendary five-finned whale Kagwaii. "He's as big as ten sperm whales," he told Gu·uu.

Da·axiigang had long intended to carve Kagwaii in a shaft of black slate, even if it was useless! Now he could feel the spirit of the legendary sea monster, so that he would carve him in all his supernatural strength and ferocity. He gave himself up to the power he could feel rushing towards him.

They swept into the Pacific.

Da·axiigang thrilled to the rage of the ocean spirits as they hurled their green-and-white fury against unyielding rock and forest. Their roar obliterated all other sound for some time.

Moving south and then east into another channel, the canoe came close to a sea lion cave. There a different roar widened Gu·uu's eyes again.

Scores of sea lions basked offshore, awash like a float of kelp. Several swam towards the cave and let the surf hurl them onto the rocks. There they romped awkwardly until they realized they preferred the sea. They gallumphed their glossy bodies back to the water's edge to catch a giant wave and let it launch them into the deep once more.

Where the swells broke on one rock, the spume became a rainbow. "The sea is dressing up for our visit," the big boy told the little boy. "And see! It's dancing for us, Gu·uu. For are we not mighty princes?" He reached the camping spot exhausted by his own reactions to the power of the Ocean People. But his artist's mind and heart were stored with riches.

The gold quartz was along a minor inlet guarded by sentry rocks. It was in a vein up a precipitous cliff. Next day, they anchored and crosstied the canoe securely below the cliff. They left Gu·uu in it, also anchored and securely crosstied, though he had freedom to move about.

The woman was first up the cliff, Da·axiigang second. "Hurry! Hurry!" he shouted down to the others. There was a wide white vein; in it were chunks of pure yellow metal.

Using fire and cold water to crack the quartz, they grubbed out a big basketful, which the slaves carried down the cliff and emptied into the canoe.

Gu·uu was enchanted with the pretty rocks. But he grew bored with them by and by, and went back to watching the flounders and bullheads that darted about below. He thought of a lovely game. He would stone the fish and kill them; they would float up to the surface, and his parents would be delighted with their fisherman. He grew red-faced and hot lugging and hoisting his heavy missiles, but he was happy. Everybody would be so pleased with him!

His grunts, his shrieks, and the splash of gold quartz and pure gold were lost in the sounds of sea, seagulls, ravens, and in the bangings of the gold miners.

The gold party returned to the canoe hot, dirty, and weary, but jubilant, jubilant until they looked into the canoe.

"Where's the first load?" the chief demanded. His eyes narrowed on his little son.

Gu·uu was tired enough now to be readily tearful. "I . . . I throwed the stones," he admitted. "I tried to get fish for you."

"Fish!" The chief grabbed for his fish club. But reason and his wife prevailed. The Haida did not strike children.

Yet Gu·uu was desolated. Tears welled in his eyes; his small chin quivered.

Da·axiigang could not bear to see him so shamed and so unhappy. "Maybe the sea spirits are pleased with a gift of gold," he suggested, squatting down by the child.

Gu·uu nodded gratefully as tears trickled down his cheeks.

"I doubt Gu·uu presented the gift with pleasing reverence," the chief commented sharply. The best chunks of pure gold had been in the first load.

"Then we'll add the reverence now, and placate offended spirits," the youth announced. He put ceremonial eagle-down into Gu·uu's fat, grubby fingers. He conducted the graceful ritual.

As 7idansuu watched the two, his eyes softened into tenderness. Then they swept wistfully over Da·axiigang's too-slender frame.

"Now the spirits are happy! Aren't they happy, Da·axiigang?" Gu·uu was pleading. "And I'm a good boy! Aren't I a good boy, Da·axiigang?"

"You are a prince," the other told him proudly. "Bold to speak the truth. Reverent to please the spirits. You are a prince, Gu·uu."

And you're a prince, Da·axiigang, his uncle thought, watching him. His heir would be a good chief, if he lived to become a chief. This lad had a feeling heart. He would care about the people. He would support their dignity.

They took the quartz to Fort Simpson where Chief Trader Kennedy was delighted to pay with blankets. He wanted to send in an exploration party, he said.

7idansuu frowned. Families who owned the site would have to agree, he warned. Even he would have to pay them for what he had taken, once ownership had been established. However, he did undertake to open negotiations for Chief Trader Kennedy at the winter potlatch.

The following summer in July 1851, the Company's brigantine *Una* sailed into the little inlet. And though pretending to be mainly interested in fur trading, Company men managed to secure sixty ounces of gold, principally by barter. They were disappointed that one Haida would not sell them a lump of pure gold weighing one pound and eleven ounces for less than 1,500 blankets. The Haida were too arrogant!

On the *Una*'s second venture that summer, Company miners were more aggressive. They took out $75,000 worth of gold under the noses of an increasingly hostile group of Haida.

Oddly enough, the *Una* sank en route to Fort Victoria, the Company's post on the southern tip of Vancouver Island.

Word of the sinking, and of the gold the *Una* had carried, raced southward to California.

This northern gold was associated with white quartz rock

similar to the auriferous deposits of California. When word of it reached the 49ers, a new gold rush was on.

But this gold rush was instantly repelled by the outraged Haida. Haida Gwaii was their land. Its gold was their gold to barter, if they chose to barter.

Haida hostility, as well as the stormy moat around the Haida islands, discouraged American miners. Nevertheless, James Douglas, chief factor for the Hudson's Bay Company's western district and governor of the little colony of Vancouver Island, advised Her Majesty Queen Victoria that it would be well to maintain a gunboat on the northwest coast to protect British rights.

The Haida did not acknowledge British rights. When the Company sent its schooner *Recovery* in with a group of Company miners in 1852, it was thwarted. The Haida simply waited for the white men to blast. Then they rushed in and grabbed the treasure. It was their gold. Let anyone else try to take it!

Chief 7idansuu became alarmed by the surge of hostility towards the Iron Men, both King George men and Boston men, that had followed the golden bullet.

He felt hostility himself. Iron Men seemed to him to be remarkably deficient in both wisdom and a sense of justice. They stood ruthlessly behind their cannons. They never learned that blasting a native village merely started a vicious cycle. They never understood that revenge was a sacred duty; that ghosts must be eased on their way to the Land of Souls; that other people had rights!

What had happened to Koyah would happen again, if both sides were not very careful. Sparks of hatred fanned so swiftly into a flame. Flames could wipe out a village, all the villages in Haida Gwaii! Maybe Iron Men would wipe out the villages for their God, who did not like totem poles.

Kwanduhadgaa's vision still haunted him.

Chief 7idansuu and his people had moved to X̱ung but were visiting Skidegate early that fall when the *Susan Sturgis* sailed in. A small trading schooner from San Francisco, the *Susan Sturgis* had $1,500 in gold on board, as well as furs and a good supply of trade goods. She was bound north to buy flake gold from a Sdast'a·aas village. Then she would round Rose Spit and call at Massett and the other north coast villages.

Chief 7idansuu dispatched a canoe to tell his people to be ready. He also talked to Captain Rooney.

"Have you ever sailed around Rose Spit, Captain?" he asked in the Chinook trade jargon, developed by the traders from native, English, and French words.

"Not yet, Chief, but I've heard about it."

Rose Spit was a ships' graveyard. Called Niikun (Nose Point) by the Haida, it jutted far into the sea at the northeastern tip of the Charlottes; and it extended even farther as a submerged and ever-changing sandbar built up and shifted by the meeting of the tides around the big group of islands. Here the currents were treacherous, the tide rips lethal, and the undertow full of power. Here, the Haida claimed, lived the most dreaded of all the storm spirits and sea monsters.

Haida canoes always stood well off the point, especially when a calm sea concealed shallows and currents. Paddlers scattered swan's-down reverently on the waters. Not even a child laughed, for fear of offending spirits. And no man ever, ever, spat in the ocean.

Iron Men were more careless about standing well out to sea. They also had deep keels on their sailing ships. In consequence, derelicts rolled like beached whales where the tides met at Rose Spit; and, like beached whales, they became the property of the nearest chief.

"Would you consider piloting me around the spit, Chief?" Captain Rooney enquired. "I'd like to have you," he coaxed, "you and your family." With the Haida as stormy as their waters, it would be well to have a leading Haida with him, he thought.

7idansuu considered. Better relations with the Iron Men should be cultivated. Besides, he liked sailing on a schooner. And so did Gu·uu. He agreed to go as pilot.

They sailed north, and rounded the spit without difficulty. It was when they were tacking west towards Massett and were near the shore that they saw canoes dart out.

"7wii·aa!" 7idansuu was aghast at the chant he heard, a war chant! And the faces had all been blackened.

These days, Chief 7wii·aa's marriage alliance with Chief Lagaahl's family at Fort Simpson contributed to his already great prestige.

Kwanduhadgaa's vision, that Massett would survive, seemed to have been all that was needed to confirm Chief 7wii·aa in his position. That and his Ƙingii pole.

Now 7idansuu's eyes narrowed on the war canoes. Chief 7wii·aa was going to be even more surprised to see 7idansuu than 7idansuu had been to see him.

"Captain," he ordered, "you and your crew go into a cabin and stay there!"

"But—" Captain Rooney was indignant. Then he was suspicious. He braced himself for battle.

"I will not have bloodshed, Captain. That is a war party."

The white man's eyes blazed. "You sent a canoe ahead," he accused. His eyes sought his cannons.

"No!" The Haida tone brooked no disobedience. "You will not shell Haida! But neither will you be harmed. I give you a chief's word."

Captain Rooney looked again at the canoes. He considered his crew of ten men. He seemed still to be uncertain.

"I will not have bloodshed," the chief repeated. "You and your crew must stay in a locked cabin."

The captain glared at him. He opened his mouth to shout to his gunners. Then he closed it instead. He ordered the crew's retreat.

Chief 7wii·aa and his warriors swarmed aboard the *Susan Sturgis* only to find Chief 7idansuu, his wife, his small son, and their several attendants standing with their backs against a closed door.

The men fell back in dismay.

Chief 7wii·aa did not fall back. "I have captured this ship," he announced. "I claim the Boston men as my captives. And I am chief in these waters." He pointed towards Massett.

"I am chief on this ship," 7idansuu retorted. "I accepted responsibility for taking this ship safely to the north coast of Haida Gwaii. And the word of a chief can't be broken."

7wii·aa lifted his dagger as if to strike.

"I'm your blood brother," the chief said, reminding him of a sacred taboo.

Chief 7wii·aa scowled at his blood brother. His eyes narrowed on 7idansuu's wife and son. They were not blood relatives; they were Kaigani Ravens.

"Touch them and launch civil war!" the chief warned him. "Every Kaigani warrior and every Haida Raven would come to tear your heart from your body."

It was an impasse.

For seven hours, while the *Susan Sturgis* drifted, Chief 7wii·aa stood there waiting. For seven hours, the Sdast'a·aas held steady.

Finally the ship ran aground near Massett.

"Now!" 7wii·aa cried out in triumph. "You can't deny that the ship is legally mine. I demand the Boston men as my captives. And now that the ship has safely reached the north coast of Haida Gwaii, Chief, your word no longer binds you to them."

"They have my word they won't be harmed," 7idansuu countered. "And they won't be harmed," he thundered.

Chief 7wii·aa's eyes glittered dangerously. "You are a leading chief; you must uphold Haida law," he insisted. "And by law this ship is mine. It has drifted onto my beach."

It was a moment of peril, a moment for wisdom.

The whole village of Massett was watching; most of the watchers were not Sdast'a·aas Eagles; most were hostile to white men.

"7wii·aa," 7idansuu quietly said, "I won't see you shamed before the other chiefs of your village."

7wii·aa's eyes glinted with triumph. His chest lifted.

"But neither will I let you drag Sdast'a·aas Eagles into warfare with the Iron Men."

7wii·aa's face fell. His eyes waited.

"Nor will I break my word to the captain . . . 7wii·aa, when I have your word that you won't harm the Boston men, I'll permit you to take them to Big House. If you agree not to harm them, I'll negotiate with the Iron Men at Fort Simpson to pay you a ransom. But if there's one scratch on one body, I'll wipe that scratch out with your blood."

"I give you the word of a chief," 7wii·aa said. "I won't harm the Boston men." He took Captain Rooney and the crew of the *Susan Sturgis* to Big House; and he led them proudly in through his Ꮶingii portal pole.

7idansuu dispatched a canoe to Fort Simpson with the news of the captives being held for ransom.

While he waited for its return, he saw 7wii·aa loot and burn the *Susan Sturgis,* but he could not legally stop it.

Then 7idansuu's messenger arrived back from Fort Simpson, with many canoes and many blankets.

Now 7idansuu announced that the Iron Men at Fort Simpson had agreed to pay $250 worth of Hudson's Bay blankets for each of the officers; $30 worth for each ordinary seaman. His men laid the payment down before 7wii·aa.

Chief 7idansuu started immediately for the mainland with the newly purchased "slaves." He handed them over to Chief Trader Kennedy at Fort Simpson with few explanations. And with only perfunctory courtesy he accepted Captain Rooney's testimonial to him:

Fort Simpson, October 10, 1852.

The bearer of this, Edenshaw, is chief of the tribe of Indians residing on North Island. I have reason to know that he is a good man, for he has been the means of saving the lives of me and my crew, who were attacked by the Massett Indians off the harbor of that name. He and his wife and child were on board that vessel coming from Skidegate harbor round to North Island, when on September 28th, 1852, we were surprised by some canoes along-side. We were so overpowered by numbers, and so sudden the attack, that all resistance on our part was quite impossible, but after gaining the cabin, this man and his wife and two or three of his men . . . protected us for seven hours until he made some terms with them for our safety. He saved my chronometer and several other things, which he brought to Fort Simpson, and gave to me, without ever asking for any remuneration. I hope if this should be shown to any master of a ship, that he will treat him well, for he deserves well at the hands of every white man.

Matthew Rooney
Former Master of the schooner *Susan Sturgis*

Word of the attack on the *Susan Sturgis* raced southward along the coast. White men called 7wii·aa a scoundrel. They decided that "Edenshaw" was probably a fellow scoundrel. No doubt he had set the whole thing up and had then turned traitor to his own people. You simply could not trust any of these treacherous bloodthirsty Haida. Everyone knew them for what they were, the most savage of the savage!

Governor Douglas was so alarmed by the *Susan Sturgis* affair that he dispatched a naval vessel to the Queen Charlotte Islands to investigate. And when Captain Prevost returned to Victoria, he reported that Chief 7idansuu was a very influential Haida whose wisdom should be heeded, even consulted, and whose authority should be supported.

Before he left Kung, Captain Prevost had presented a gift to Gu·uu. It was a New Testament inscribed "To the Indian Boy, Edensaw's son. I trust that the bread cast upon the waters will soon be found."

This *Book* startled Gu·uu's father with the remembrance of Mr. Green's *Book* at Kaigani more than twenty years earlier. It, too, was an unnerving packet of rustling ghost leaves. It, too, undoubtedly said that God did not like totem poles.

7idansuu banished the *Book* promptly to a carved cedar chest; but he could not banish the picture it conjured up, the vision of Kwanduhadgaa.

All the Haida villages were going to be wiped out, except Massett and Skidegate.

S E V E N

AFTER THE *SUSAN STURGIS* AFFAIR, hostility towards white traders tended to increase. Visits by British gunboats brought scowls. Yet the foreign trade had become increasingly important to the Sdast'a·aas.

"I should have gone to England," Chief 7idansuu said ruefully to his heir one day. "I should have gone to England and married the queen's daughter." Marriage was the surest way to cement friendly trade relations. Most high chiefs had several wives, each the relative of some powerful neighbor. "I had the chance, Da·axiigang. I should have gone to England."

Chief 7idansuu was a handsome man. And in him the innate stateliness of the Haida was enhanced by generations of command. When he donned a black sea otter cloak and a canoe hat painted with his crest, he was an imposing figure. In his ceremonial robes, deeply fringed Chilkat blanket and crestal crown ringed with sea lion bristles and hung with ermine skins, he was truly a chief.

Once, seeing him in full regalia, an English sea captain had invited him to London.

"You would cut quite a figure there," he had said admiringly. "No doubt the queen would receive you. And by Jove, man, you could marry a queen's daughter." He had meant that last as a flattering jest.

"I was invited to go," the chief recalled wistfully. "And I should have gone, Da·aẋiigang. My refusal to go may even have offended the queen."

"Then go now!" Da·aẋiigang proposed. "Uncle," he urged, "you go to the head village of the King George men; and I'll go to the head village of the Boston men, and marry a Boston princess. Then we'll have good relations with both main nations of Iron Men. And," he added with gleeful spite, "we'll put 7wii·aa in his place."

His eyes sparkled. All his life Da·aẋiigang had wanted to go to Boston. Of all the Iron Men, he liked best the whaling men who wintered at Skidegate. He always wanted to hold his nose like a sleeping sea otter when he boarded a whaler, but whaling men were his kind of men. They carved. They were always carving whalebone or whale teeth or coconut husks. The things they carved were beyond his comprehension: jagging wheels, picture frames, busks. In Chinook jargon and pantomime, they explained "pie crimping" and "ladies' stays"; and when he still smiled in bafflement, they generously swept all their carved articles into one word, scrimshaw.

"Scrimshaw!" He uttered the magic word now. And it was magic. It had changed all his useless slate carvings into a brisk trade item. Now when he sculpted a small figure that had no use beyond training his hand and delighting his own eyes, Iron Men competed to buy it. For some curious reason, they called his work "curios," and whalermen's work "scrimshaw."

"I'd love to go to a Boston potlatch," he confessed to his uncle. He could see the feasthouse and the blazing fire. He could envision the piles of blankets, muskets, and iron pots, and the mounds of scrimshaw. "A Boston potlatch!" he repeated wistfully, imagining his wedding to a Boston princess. "And why not?" he demanded of his uncle. "I could go in a whaler."

"Well . . . someday, perhaps," Chief 7idansuu agreed, not letting his tone betray his doubt that the young man was equal to such a journey. "At present you are too valuable to be spared, stimulating the trade in curios."

———————

Now sixteen and living in his uncle's house, Da·ax̱iigang frequently went back to Skidegate, traveling by sea since there were practically no trails through the timbered mountains and the muskeg swamps of Haida Gwaii.

For him, slate was the lure. The beautiful black argillite was found only on Slatechuck Mountain, up a creek near Skidegate. It belonged to the people of Skidegate, so he had to pay for it. And though he had slaves to pack out the heavy rock, he climbed the rugged terrain himself to select and supervise the cutting out of his pieces.

Slate carvers at Skidegate watched his work with fascinated eyes. He was audacious. He did new and startling things with traditional patterns. More highly skilled, older craftsmen than he caught inspiration from him, even while they were teaching him how to achieve the dramatic emphasis of the identifying symbol and the perfect finish that distinguished all Haida work.

Among the Haida, art was a profession for the high born. A carver brought to his work the pride of a high position, and also the refined taste of a man who had never touched a paddle or a fish club that was not elegantly decorated. If a lesser man showed talent, he might be trained; but if he carved a totem pole for a chief, the pole bore the ceremonial adze cut of some highborn carver to make it acceptable. Art was immensely honored. For only through his richly ornamented house, his crest poles, his decorated canoes, tools, and household goods, and his dancing regalia, could a chief demonstrate his distinction. And, since a chief's prestige was shared by his people, every villager was intensely concerned with the quality of each bit of decoration. Every Haida was an art connoisseur. Every Haida man carved his own fish club, painted his own storage boxes. Thus Da·axiigang's natural genius was stimulated by an art-oriented society.

With his talent went proud confidence. The heir to the chieftainship of the Sdast'a·aas Eagles dared to do what he wished. He was not cowed by a startled frown. He was not limited by tradition. Chiefs were the makers of new tradition.

Also freeing him as an innovator was his new medium and his new market. Slate was not bound by the customs of centuries. Curio buyers were unaware of traditional restrictions. Applied art could suddenly blossom into pure art, and yet still contribute to the material good of the people.

Scrimshaw changed relief carving into statuary.

Even his lack of physical robustness helped to free the artist in Da·axiigang. While other carvers must also be sea hunters and fishermen and warriors, he could be just an artist. He enjoyed dedication. His work showed the quality achieved only by the unremitting practice of an art.

And while he chipped away happily in an isolated village, whispers of the discovery of a great new artist were beginning to spread through the salons of Europe.

"Indian work?" critics exclaimed as they scrutinized sculptures that were miniature, yet monumental in power. They ran appreciative fingers over stone that had the sheen of black satin. This work was unique. "Primitive art!" they said. "But this is highly sophisticated. It's the work of a cultured professional." It was, some of them contended, much, much more developed than African art, much more highly evolved than Polynesian. It must have taken thousands of years to develop a monumentality that could not be defeated by size. "Reduce even Michelangelo to three inches," one commented, "and his David would be a doll." Yet a three-inch Haida sculpture was full of power.

The argillite pieces gave new excitement to their study of the Haida. No other nation on the whole continent produced these exquisite black sculptures. Sea captains were commissioned to pick up Haida carvings for important collections; and though none of the work was signed, they were to try especially hard to find the powerful pieces some young chieftain was doing.

The eagerness of the buyers in turn stimulated the carvers. Their work became even better. And their interest in their own legends increased, for mythology was the fountainhead of their art motifs.

Almost forgotten tales were grubbed out, like slate; and like slate, they were worked over, polished, and then handsomely presented. Winter potlatches attained an unheard of brillance in Haida lodges. People could almost forget the vision of Kwanduhadgaa.

Then, in 1857, gold was discovered in the sands of the Fraser River, in Salish lands on the mainland, just north of the Oregon Country.

During the summer of 1858, 33,000 men rushed north from San Francisco. They docked first at Fort Victoria on the southern tip of Vancouver Island. And here the Hudson's Bay Company's James Douglas became alarmed at the extent of the American invasion.

With his help, Her Britannic Majesty moved fast. She proclaimed the whole wilderness the Gold Colony of British Columbia. Magistrates and policemen were sworn in to enforce English law. Soldiers arrived from England. Royal Navy gunboats patrolled the waters. Miners' licenses were imposed to emphasize British possession.

The Haida, as curious as the rest of the local residents, paddled the six hundred miles south to see if all the fantastic rumors could be true. The *British Colonist* reported their arrival at Victoria in its April 23rd issue, 1859:

HAIDAH INDIANS—About eighty canoes containing nearly 1,000 Indians arrived on Thursday from Queen Charlotte's Island. They have pitched their lodges at the north end of the town. They have brought several very fine specimens of gold-bearing quartz and some fine gold. We are not informed as to what part of the Island they obtained their gold from.

The fine gold was from the northern part.

"Why did you bring gold here?" Chief 7idansuu demanded of Massett Town Chief 7wii·aa when he heard the report.

"The Skidegate brought gold quartz," 7wii·aa countered.

"Do they want this to come to Haida Gwaii?" 7idansuu exclaimed, encompassing Victoria with a sweep of his arm.

This was a tent town full of Iron Men, saloons, and muddy streets. This was crowded ships arriving from San Francisco, and even more crowded ships leaving for the diggings on the mainland. Worst of all, this was a fringe of native encampments exploited by the whisky trader. In the native camps, burned out ancient feuds were being rekindled by firewater. A drunk Tlingit stabbed a drunk Haida. A drunk Haida boy shot a staggering Stikine (Tlingit) boy. Indignant Tlingit and Haida families retaliated with daggers and muskets. The old rivalries of the three northern nations of coast native people were reactivated.

7idansuu and Da·a×iigang were shaken by the sight of dirty, murderous louts who had recently been handsome Skidegate youths.

"It's like Yaahl's curse," Da·a×iigang observed to his uncle. "Once they have tasted whisky, they can't stop their greed for it. They're possessed by its evil spirits. It shames them deeply, yet they can't resist it. Like Raven!" It was so even with women and children, he saw.

This was an outrage not to be borne meekly.

"By what right do the King George men claim this land?" 7idansuu demanded of Governor Douglas. "There are no treaties. There was no conquest by warriors."

"It was forced on us by the gold rush," the governor explained. "I'll do all I can to protect Indian rights."

"Then stop the whisky traders!"

The governor did not, or could not, stop the infamous traffic. And it was not even good whisky. A young English engineer protested in print against the "soul destroying stuff":

The so-called whiskey which is shamelessly sold to the Indians by certain unprincipled merchants at Victoria contains very little of what is wholesome or genuine liquor. Its strength proceeds wholly from the blue-stone vitriol and nitric acids which the manufacturers largely infuse into it. The consequence is that their naturally fiery temperaments are wrought up into a state of savagery so intense as to leave no white man's life safe.

The "state of savagery" was far more destructive of native life. And, as Da·axiigang had observed, it was like Raven's curse of gluttony.

"That's Raven's cry," he burst out angrily as he listened to relatives wailing for the death of a fourteen-year-old drunk. He wrenched his thoughts away from the terrible whisky.

"By what right do Boston men and King George men take Salish gold?" he went on. Then he added with ferocious glee. "They didn't take Haida gold!"

Uncle and nephew seethed with indignation on behalf of those weaker nations whose rights they themselves had not altogether respected.

"But that was different," they assured one another. They had simply obeyed the prevailing law of life: the strong used the weak. They had even been merciful in following this law. They had avoided bloodshed. They had made stealthy raids to snatch slaves; then they had treated the slaves so humanely that most became devoted servants. "Better a slave in a Haida village than a skeleton at home," some said, shrugging. A slave was the single most valuable piece of property a Haida could have; such Haida property was kept valuable by good food and good treatment.

"This is a new tribe of Boston men," Da·axiigang continued anxiously. "They're not like the friendly whaling men. Don't you notice how they eye us as if we were hovering sharks?"

And indeed the gold-seekers did eye every native person with hostility and suspicion. Newly arrived from their own territories where "Indian wars" were raging, Americans saw in every native person the treacherous blood-brother of the Sioux, Apache, Paiute, or Commanche warrior. At best, he was "a gol-darn nuisance" to men who only wanted to get in, get rich, and then get out fast with their skins unpunctured.

In turn, the native people saw every gold-seeker as a rude trespasser who, unlike a proper man, did not come with an affectionate family. He came alone, to grab. And he grabbed women as well as gold, after he had degraded them with firewater.

"If we are helpless against a curse, like Raven," Da·ax̱iigang suggested, "maybe we, too, should banish ourselves."

Greatly perturbed by what had happened to their coast, he and his uncle went back with their people to clean, remote K'yuusdaa.

But the gold rush was a lure. No one could resist paddling south to see what else was happening. The following spring, fleets of Haida canoes made their way again through the islands that fringe the Inside Passage to Victoria.

Chief 7idansuu did not risk taking many people south with him that spring of 1860. And he was aghast at the numbers of the Skidegate he found there, and at the numbers of Kaigani, Tsimshian, Tongas, and Stikine (Tlingit); all neighbors from the north.

He was even more aghast at the intertribal feuding activated by firewater. More than ever before, futile rage against the overpowering white man turned on fellow native people. Understandably, it turned most fiercely on the Haida, the lords of the coast. Centuries of resentment burst out, especially among the northern neighbors.

On May 26th, colony policemen forcibly quelled a riot between Haida drunks and a combined group of Tongas and Stikine.

Three days later a Tongas chief threw a knife to kill the favorite dog of Captain John, a famous Haida with Russian blood. Captain John sent a slave out to kill the Tongas chief.

In retaliation, the Stikine shot two Haida.

A dead Stikine was found floating in the bay.

Barricades were being erected for war.

British sailors from the nearby Pacific station at Esquimalt stepped in with guns and whips; gunboats stood offshore, their cannons trained on the native encampments.

The native people raged with resentment at these white men; but the rage turned on their ancient rivals. On June 12th, a thousand Haida reinforcements arrived at Victoria.

Alarmed at the thought of what might happen next, Governor Douglas tried to banish all the natives with a measles scare, which had often worked before. But the native people weren't frightened by it now. So he called in the chiefs.

"Go home!" he implored them.

"We'll go home when we're ready," they retorted.

"Then forget your ancient enmities!" he pleaded. "And forget your blood code! If you have a grievance against another Indian, let the police punish him!"

A wily Stikine instantly demanded the arrest of Captain John for the murder of the Tongas chief.

Governor Douglas had to make good his word. He sent the entire police force and Royal Marines to arrest Captain John. But the Haida would not give him up. Troops cowed them with a show of steel; they confiscated muskets and pistols; they rounded up riot leaders; and they flogged the leaders in public. Then they bore Captain John off in triumph.

He could not endure the indignity of being searched for weapons. He would not endure the shame of captivity. He made a wild break for freedom, and was shot down.

The Haida prepared to attack Victoria.

Somehow, Governor Douglas and head chiefs like 7idansuu managed to prevent open war. And the natives scattered.

Reporting on the departure of the terrible Haida, the *British Colonist* predicted:

"Now the Hydahs will be more manageable . . . or else start a war of annihilation."

The Sdast'a·aas went home heartsick, grieving for handsome, lovable, swashbuckling Captain John who had been to London and Petrograd and Acapulco.

Captain John's son, a young Kaigani chief, went home too, swearing vengeance on all white men. "Let any of them dare to come again to Kaigani!" he muttered.

Chief 7idansuu visited all the Sdast'a·aas in their home villages. He spoke to the people, warning them against Victoria.

And the power of his words was still stronger than the pull of the gold rush. Few Sdast'a·aas went south in 1861. Instead, the tap, tap of little finishing adzes could be heard all day long as men shaped graceful canoes or carved storage boxes. Shouts of children filled sunlit northern evenings with merriment as they played tag on the beach, or counted points won for driving their team's spears into the other side's squares of spruce bark.

"Tonight my heart feels good," 7idansuu remarked to his heir one peaceful evening.

"And my heart feels good!" Da·axiigang answered with unexpected gusto. "Uncle! I've just had a stupendous idea for a new kind of curio."

He had been gazing absent-mindedly at the Raven story pole at the corner of their house when he had idly thought, "If only the pole were glossy black, like Raven!"

"Polished slate poles!" he said now. "Why not make miniature totem poles in black slate?"

The chief considered. Then his eyes too sparkled with an artist's excitement. "A miniature story pole for every episode

119

in the Raven tale," he enthusiastically suggested. "Da·axiigang, you're a genius!"

"I'm a genius," his heir agreed blithely. "I'll make the first one like this house pole, 'Raven and the Halibut Fisherman.' Then . . . 'Raven and Old Tsing, the Beaver.'"

He could hardly sleep that night. He kept seeing one story pole after another, with the figures of the characters placed one above another, as in the big totem poles. At daybreak he was started on the stimulating project.

He planned a sculpture in his head. And not until every inch of his design was visible to his mind's eye did he start to carve. Then, like all Haida, he roughed out his work with an assurance that would have seemed reckless to a white man.

Actually, his slate poles were not mere replicas of totem poles. Their proportions were revolutionary. Tall wooden totem poles were relief carving applied to a column; Da·axiigang's little slate poles were sculptures.

They were an instant success with both carvers and buyers. The market was so good that Da·axiigang felt he could not spare time the following summer, 1862, to accompany his uncle to Victoria to check on the progress of the gold rush.

And so it was that when Chief 7idansuu's seventy-two-foot canoe continued southward, Da·axiigang's smaller craft turned off at Skidegate.

He went first to Slatechuck Mountain for a supply of damp, raw, gray slate; then he went directly to his father's canoe-making camp in the forest. And as giant red cedars were felled and roughly shaped nearby, Da·axiigang chatted happily with relatives between sessions of concentrated carving.

Chief 7idansuu was again heartsick at the degradation he found in the native encampments around Victoria. He could not shame other chiefs, however, by telling them to go home.

"It's like this everywhere, 7idansuu," an old, old chief said to him sadly. "The whisky traders go up and down the coast now."

"Stop the whisky traders!" 7idansuu again implored the governor.

"I haven't enough policemen," the governor pleaded. "There's too much to cope with, too suddenly, and not enough money for hiring people."

Suddenly the governor sent an urgent summons to all the chiefs encamped near Victoria. "A man arrived from San Francisco with smallpox," he told them. "An epidemic is sweeping the town. Go home! Take your people back to their villages!"

"Smallpox?" a chief retorted contemptuously. "So you have finally learned that 'measles' will no longer scare us off the land you Iron Men want. Now you try 'smallpox.' "

"There is smallpox," Governor Douglas insisted.

"There's something new every year," the chief agreed. "First it was measles. Then it was rent, we must pay rent to the intruders or else go home! Now you try yet another ruse to make us obey you."

Governor Douglas, whose own wife had native as well as Irish fur-trader blood, begged them to go.

But they were adamant.

"If we obey him," they reminded one another, "we acknowledge his right to give orders to us." This situation was like a potlatch. Public acknowledgment of a claim made it valid, by the custom of the country.

They refused to go home.

"Then I will make you go home," the governor thundered at them.

He ordered out the police, the Royal Marines, and the navy

gunboats. Warning cannon shots splintered cedar huts. And while muskets and big guns held the natives at bay, canoes were tied in long lines behind navy craft; people were forced into the canoes; they were towed out of Victoria harbor, and north along the coast.

Chief 7idansuu's magnificent canoe was towed by a gunboat, with the canoes of his people.

It was an indignity not to be borne!

The chief did not bear it long. Suddenly he leapt along the canoe. He slashed the towrope. His men followed his lead, and the whole Sdast'a.aas fleet headed back for Victoria, chanting triumphantly. They landed with the traditional flourish of the Eagles. Entering the harbor, all the crews stroked in unison, without sound or ripples, symbolizing the stealthiness of an approach upon an enemy. Then, with a war cry, they dashed their paddles deep into the water in simulated attack. A paean of triumph followed. And then, like weary eagles, they nosed shoreward with two strokes, a rest; three strokes, a pause; alternating the pattern and keeping time to a chant. As they touched shore, they crossed paddles. These were the mighty Eagles! These were Haida, the lords of the coast!

They stayed only long enough to establish their right to stay. Then they chose to go home.

As they moved northward along the coast, they saw people dying. Before they reached Haida waters, people were sickening in their own canoes. And now, wanting only to put space between themselves and the new pestilence, they rushed to their hereditary haven, Haida Gwaii.

———————

Back in Haida Gwaii, a happier group — 7idansuu's young brother and his family — was leaving Massett for K'yuusdaa.

The party included his ten-year-old daughter, a girl who carried the highest bloodline of the Kaigani Ravens.

A sunny natured child, Sun-Lak-Kwee-Kun was not yet unduly aware of the decorum expected of a princess whose name meant "Most Serene Highness." She delightedly played dolls with her little "sister," her older sister's four-year-old daughter, an almost as important Kaigani Raven.

Their favorite doll was a slender creature carved from a stalactite. This doll had real hair glued on with halibut-fin cement. It had a gorgeous wardrobe of fur cloaks, tiny canoe hats, and miniature jewelry. It even had a cosmetic bag with a complexion stick cut to match the princesses' own greasesticks which, of course, had been shaped with a handle by having perfumed deer-fat solidified in a small kelp bulb.

The doll's wardrobe was the special care of Wiiba, the four-year-old's devoted slave-playmate.

After a visit to Massett, the party had left for K'yuusdaa. They had paddled westward only as far as Jalun River, however, when they saw a storm approaching. So they had camped there, to watch for good weather to continue their journey.

The two princesses and Wiiba had settled happily on the beach with their dolls. And they were only casually watched by relatives and attendants, who had all been taken sick.

Also on the north coast of Haida Gwaii that day were two uncles of the Raven princesses, one of them Kaigani Chief Kitzgalum. They were at at Massett when the infected canoes arrived. "Smallpox!" Kitzgalum gasped, shrinking away from the evil spirits. Then, in alarm, he whispered, "Sun-Lak-Kwee-Kun!"

She was on her way to K'yuusdaa, he knew. And canoes were heading that way, full of sick people!

"The vision of Kwanduhadgaa!" he muttered. The villages of Haida Gwaii were to be wiped out. But the noblest bloodline of the Kaigani Ravens must not be wiped out with them! "To K'yuusdaa! Fast!" he ordered his paddlers.

His sixty-five-foot canoe shot westward; it rushed past the other canoes.

At Jalun River, he saw the canoes of Sun-Lak-Kwee-Kun's family. Then he saw her and her "sister." He beached his canoe and leapt out.

When he was a few yards offshore, Sun-Lak-Kwee-Kun's father shouted "Smallpox!" to warn the Raven chief.

Kitzgalum snatched up the princesses, one under each mighty arm; he hoisted them into his canoe. "Push off!" he ordered his paddlers.

The princesses' fathers both made for Kitzgalum's canoe; both shouted for their daughters; both splashed through the icy waters.

"I'm taking the girls to safety," Kitzgalum told them.

"Safety?" They pointed to the storm warnings. "Look at the sky!" they entreated. "Come back or you'll drown our daughters!"

Kitzgalum faced them, ruthless. "If there are no little girls, there'll be nothing left of us," he said. "Paddle!" he ordered, grimly.

The tiny girl yelled for her father. Then she started to scream for Wiiba.

Sun-Lak-Kwee-Kun held her, and hushed her, snuggling her into a fur cloak. Blinking back her own tears, she cuddled the forlorn little figure. Uncle Kitzgalum was steering straight for Alaska, she saw. No storm at sea held such terror for him as the spirits of Kali Koustli and the vision of Kwanduhadgaa. He was fleeing Haida Gwaii, where the villages were doomed to die. She was stunned by the thought of what might happen to her parents at Jalun River. And, more and more, she was watching the blackening storm clouds.

The sea stayed calm for most of the crossing. Great snowy peaks of Alaska were close when the wind suddenly freshened. It whipped up waves on the wide Pacific swells. It began to snatch spray from the waves; the sea became as dark as wet slate.

"We're nearly there," she kept whispering encouragingly; but her eyes widened with fear as she watched gigantic crests and troughs race through the ocean. She added her prayers to her uncle's as a woman scattered eagle-down on the waters. She watched his face as he strained to keep his high prow slicing into wild seas.

The girls huddled together. Each time the canoe climbed the crest of a wave, the crest ahead flung spume at them, stinging their eyes and faces.

In grim silence, the paddlers plied their blades. In the shelter of each trough, they had a moment's respite. Then they dug in their paddles, while icy water drenched them. And they managed to reach shore just before the gale set the sea really to smoking. They fell exhausted on the beach, while people rushed up to help them.

"We're here!" Sun-Lak-Kwee-Kun wearily murmured, hugging her little "sister." "We're . . . home," she added, blinking back hot tears.

The two girls were orphans before that summer was over. The entire camping group at Jalun River was wiped out by smallpox.

Chief 7idansuu escaped it, as did his wife and young son Gu·uu. A few of his villagers also survived contact with the dread disease. Then other villagers returned from isolated fishing camps, or, like Da·aӿiigang, from canoe-making camps in the forest.

Altogether, only eighty people survived at Ҟung, where

there had been over three hundred. The grave house at the end of the village was bursting with corpses. Gigantic cedar houses echoed with emptiness. Ghosts wailed with the sea winds that tore at tree branches.

It was the same in every village. Where hundreds had lived, now there were only dozens.

"God did not like totem poles," people murmured everywhere, stunned by the terrible punishment He had meted out to them.

And the ghosts wailed in the wind.

It was better that the ghosts stay near the villages, people decided. If they left, God would only pitch them into the burning lake where they would scream to die; but He would never let them die because He was punishing them for the totem poles.

God did not like the smell of corpses in the mortuary poles, either, they remembered.

Now, the breeze sometimes carried an unbearable stench.

During the desolate winter, the winds howled, and the ghosts wailed and wailed and wailed around the lonely village.

When spring came, women pleaded with sea hunters not to go out for sea lions. "What if you should drown," they asked, "when we have so few men left?"

Never before had Haida women shown fear for their bold sea hunters.

The vision of Kwanduhadgaa was coming true. That was what haunted 7idansuu. God was wiping out the villages. So the rest must be true also. Totem poles, recording a legendary history, must be graven images as Mr. Green had told him; and, somehow, graven images were evil.

It was beyond belief that totem poles could be evil.

Yet, how could he not believe it?

The chief and his heir discussed it a thousand times. God was wiping out the villages, so the totem poles must be evil.

They tried to help their people. "More canoes!" they urged, striving to keep minds occupied with work. They told stories to cheer the people, especially stories of how their valiant ancestors had survived many catastrophes. Even the Flood. But perhaps the stories were evil, too.

"No!" said Da·aꭓiigang. "The stories are not evil. And totem poles are not evil, either." Every time he carved another beautiful little black totem pole, he knew that they were not evil.

Away from Haida Gwaii, white men heard of the smallpox epidemic; but they did not understand what a catastrophe it was. They did not realize that a great culture was dying from shock. In fact, few suspected there was a culture to die.

Seventy years earlier, when Captain Dixon sailed joyously out of Cloak Bay with a wealth of sea otter skins, there had been ten thousand healthy Haida in thriving villages all around the coasts of their isolated islands.

Now there were only a thousand.

"Sdast'a·aas means ever-increasing, like maggots," the chief reminded his Eagles. Their very name was a promise that they would be great again, he assured them.

Alone, he wept.

E I G H T

LATER, CHIEF 7IDANSUU MENTIONED THE GOLD RUSH CITY of Victoria to his heir. "If I had obeyed the governor," he said ruefully, "perhaps . . ." His voice died away in anguish.

"Native chiefs can't obey a foreign intruder," Da·axiigang protested. "We can't acknowledge his right to command us."

"Unless we give him that right. I've been thinking," said Chief 7idansuu. "The governor has a feeling heart. And there's native blood in his family. Even his name is one honored in our lineage. I think, if he had more power, he'd stand up to the whisky traders." He gazed long and silently at the sea. "So I've decided to give him more power among the chiefs."

To do this, Chief 7idansuu went south to Victoria. He talked earnestly about smallpox, whisky traders, native lands, and other matters of vital, mutual interest. Then he presented many gifts to make the governor wealthier and more important in native eyes.

"And now I'll raise a pole to him," he announced on his return to the village. "He's the best Iron Man I ever met."

Unfortunately, Governor Douglas retired that year, though not before making a strong case for generous treatment of native people, or before setting aside many reserves. The queen had honored him with a knighthood.

The Haida honored him with a more unique tribute, a totem pole. Since Sir James Douglas appeared to own no personal crests, however, the Haida had to do what they could. They decided that his identifying symbol was his top hat; and 7idansuu contented himself with carving a lifelike figure of the ex-governor in frock coat and top hat at the top of a bare cedar pole.

He raised it with ceremony. And his people, caught up in this ancient ceremony of pole-raising, cheered as the Haida had always cheered. Their numbness was passing at last. The old cycle of springtime and geese, summer and wild roses, autumn and the salmon runs, winter and winter gales, was healing shattered spirits.

———

Da·axiigang did more for his people than he knew. When they saw his eager face glowing above some exquisite new slate pole, they found their fears lifting like sea mists in the morning sun. They knew in their hearts that their totem poles were not evil. They wanted only to dismiss the catastrophe from their minds, and to live as they had always lived. Old customs were as reassuring as the old, reliable rhythm of the seasons.

Only men like Chief 7idansuu recognized the shallowness of the reassurance. The pride of the Haida had been broken. A baffling sense of shame was rotting the foundations of their very life.

As soon as the raven cried each morning, they were up and busy, repairing their lives. They harvested the sea and the seashore and the berry swamps and the forest. They chipped, chipped, chipped at fragrant cedars to shape canoes for the trade.

But there was an emptiness.

Some men filled the emptiness with ambition. Many chieftainships were now vacant; great names waited for new wearers.

"We're all descended from Copper Woman," ambitious Eagles pointed out.

"And we're all descended from Foam Woman," ambitious Ravens noted.

Any man in the proper family could claim one of its chieftainships or its famous names. He could make his claim valid only by public acceptance of it at a potlatch. If he could become wealthy enough to give a potlatch; if people would accept his gifts, and so his claim, at that potlatch; if he could pay for the carving and the raising of a pole bearing the crests he now laid claim to, he could become a noble.

Ambition proved as infectious as smallpox had been. Men in some families other than the tightly controlled Sdast'a·aas families even sold wives and daughters into a life of shame in the gold camps to get wealth for their potlatches; ambitious women offered to go. Contenders served whisky at their feasts to lure the witnesses they needed.

All along the northwest coast of North America, competing totem poles rose higher and higher in the villages. After the horror of the epidemic, and perhaps in violent reaction to it, came the tragedy of the golden age of totem poles. Crest poles towered against the sky, no longer a reverent tribute to the past. Sea captains reported that native villages looked from a distance like harbors crowded with ships' masts.

True chief were dismayed at this ruinous greed for prestige. They hastened to strengthen their own ancient, honored bloodlines.

Sdast'a·aas Eagles and Kaigani Ravens consulted. The survival of the highest lineages outweighed all other considerations, certainly those of age. So arrangements were made for the marriage of Sun-Lak-Kwee-Kun. It was agreed that as soon as she emerged from the ceremonial seclusion of girlhood into the dignity of young womanhood, she would become the young, second wife of Chief 7idansuu. The younger orphaned Raven princess would be publicly proclaimed their daughter at the marriage potlatch. Then she would marry Da·axiigang when she came of age.

The pageant of a Haida state wedding took place at Kaigani in the autumn of 1870. A fleet of Sdast'a·aas canoes went to Alaska to bring their new young chieftainess home to Haida Gwaii. And 7idansuu's first wife (whose concern for their mutual Raven lineage also outweighed other considerations) folded two richly cloaked orphans to her heart. She accepted them both, like daughters. And Gu·uu, now a handsome Raven chieftain, welcomed them affectionately into the close family circle.

To 7idansuu's twelve personal slaves were now added Sun-Lak-Kwee-Kun's ten slaves. To his store of household goods were added the wedding gifts of the delighted Kaigani. The house at Ḵung was warmed with blazing fires and stories and laughter. Flickering light glinted on the lovely young chieftainess's gold earrings and bracelets and anklets, all engraved with her favorite Killer Whale crest.

Though she was merry on occasion, and though she clung wistfully to her "daughter" in private, her public decorum began to match the name that meant Most Serene Highness. And in her presence, the brash *nouveaux riches* of other clans fumbled with awkwardness. She began to be the force that strong women tend to become in a matrilineal social order.

All of this added to Chief 7idansuu's power to control his people for their own salvation. While other villages began to be dubbed "towns of sick women and totem poles," his was called "the hope of the Haida race" by the few outsiders who cared at all.

The native population was decreasing steadily now, year after year.

The government appointed a commissioner to administer the affairs of a dying race. All the land belonged to the queen, this commissioner informed the native people; but the government would give them sufficient lands for their use.

The native chiefs protested with dignity, vigor, and logic.

"What we don't like about the government is their saying this, 'We will give you this much land,' " they protested. "How can they give it when it is our own? We cannot understand it. They have never bought it from us or our forefathers. They have never fought and conquered our people and taken the land that way, and yet they say now they will give us so much land— our own land!"

The logic was unanswerable, so the government did not bother to answer.

Isolated by the wild sea, though, the Haida could assert more independence than other nations along the coast. Chief 7idansuu could devote himself mainly to domestic problems.

Town Chief 7wii·aa too had survived the epidemic, as had his relative Siigee, a spirited and highborn Raven chief, who was old Town Chief Siigee's nephew.

"Young Siigee is my hope at Massett," 7idansuu confided to Sun-Lak-Kwee-Kun. "We must have peace in Haida Gwaii. We can't afford to hurt one another."

Young Chief Siigee surged with the old spirit of the sea rover, with the old Haida joy in the ocean. He followed the now sparse and wary sea otter and seal far off to the west. He slept happily on the wide Pacific, and then roved even farther west. He had the steadiness to shoot a seal when he and his target were both heaving in a rough sea.

"He heartens all the young men," 7idansuu observed. "He gives them back their Haida pride. And he laughs away the fears of the women."

Massett was increasingly important. With its famous stand of red cedars at the head of Massett Inlet, the village was becoming "the shipyard of the north." And with its central position on the north coast of Haida Gwaii, it was drawing in the huddled remnants of neighboring villages.

Similarly, Skidegate was central on the east coast. And with its monopoly of slate—Skidegate owned the only known deposit of argillite on the coast—it was becoming the headquarters of the curio trade. It, too, was drawing in lonely remnants.

Only Massett and Skidegate would survive. People remembered this on dark, lonely nights. More and more they saw Kwanduhadgaa's vision coming true.

"Maybe we should move to Massett," people whispered even at Ḵung.

———
———

Early in the year of 1876, a ceremonial Massett messenger arrived at Ḵung. Town Chief 7wii·aa, he said, wished to scatter the eagle-down at a feast he would give in honor of the illustrious head chief of the Sdast'a·aas Eagles.

This is Siigee's doing! Chief 7idansuu thought gratefully.

The feast was set for the first blooming of the wild roses, the messenger said. Then the canoe-traders would have returned from Fort Simpson, and the clam-diggers would be back from the beaches.

Gu·uu narrowed his eyes with suspicion at this invitation. "Once before, an old Haida enemy was invited to a dance of peace in 7wii·aa's house," he pointed out.

It had been a long, long time before, with another 7wii·aa. And each visitor had arrived only to have his head lopped off as he entered through the hole in the portal pole. A supposed shout of welcome had drowned out the sound of each successive murder.

"We have nothing to fear from *this* 7wii·aa," Gu·uu's father assured him. "This peace dance is Siigee's doing. And I'm happy to go."

His happiness was short lived. Massett canoe-makers had not even left yet for Fort Simpson when Siigee was caught in a squall off Rose Spit. He and his shipwrecked crew managed to struggle ashore through the terrible surf. They managed to drag themselves up the beach ahead of the oncoming tide. But they had been too long in the numbing water.

Sickness struck at Siigee's lungs. And though the medicine man worked over him with charms and incantations, he became desperately ill. His sunken eyes burned; his cheeks flamed with fever; he coughed incessantly.

"This is the Iron Man's sickness," his anxious young wife said, recognizing the consumptive symptoms now so prevalent in native villages. "Maybe we should send for the Iron Man's sorcerer." Being a Tsimshian from the mainland, she knew of the medical work of the missionaries.

Chief 7wii·aa was reluctant to offend his own medicine man by bringing in a foreign sorcerer.

"Then I'll send for him myself," Siigee's wife told several people. And she sent for the missionary when the trade canoes went to Fort Simpson.

———

The Reverend Mr. Collison arrived in Massett in June, 1876, with the first blooming of the wild roses.

The feast had not been cancelled.

So, one day later than the missionary, Chief 7idansuu and his villagers arrived in the several war canoes that could now hold them all. The pitiful remnant came as Eagles had always come to a feast. A drummer in the leading canoe beat a proud rhythm. Paddlers stroked in patterned unison: two strokes, a pause; three strokes, a rest. And while women and children and nobles stood in the canoes, swaying with graceful motions of head and hands, all chanted the brave deeds of their valiant ancestors.

An answering chant rose from the Massett beach. Naked, blackened slaves rushed into the surf to cast coppers under Chief 7idansuu's state canoe.

Massett villagers in full dancing regalia led the way into Big House. And even Gu·uu betrayed no concern as he ducked in through the hole in the portal pole, the Kingii pole.

After guests were carefully seated on cedar mats, according to their rank, Town Chief 7wii·aa entered, preceded by his subchiefs and principal men. Shaking his bird rattle, he danced slowly around the lodge, bowing before each important visitor to waft a cloud of swan's-down, the sacred symbol that bound him and them to friendship.

"My heart feels good," Chief 7idansuu told Chief 7wii·aa and

7wii·aa's people. To crown the occasion, he performed a poignant ceremony.

During the winter storms, his uncle's (Yatz's) pole had been blown down at K'yuusdaa. One of the old-style, relatively small poles, it had been towed to Ƙung by sea hunters, and then on to Massett. Now it was carried into Big House; and while it was held upright, 7idansuu performed a strange and beautiful chief's dance before it. As his villagers chanted Yatz's story, he dramatized the youth's first sighting of the flying canoe, then the excitement of his first fur-trading, then the sadness of Maada and the tiny princeling. He pantomimed the life story of his beloved uncle. And people wept, watching him and remembering the proud old days that were dying.

When the pole was cast on the fire, its flames brightened carved house posts almost into life; its sparks rushed up through the smoke hole, and out into lonely silence.

After such a moving reminder of a common heritage, all felt a surge of friendship towards 7idansuu. They listened with affectionate respect while he echoed the protests Chief 7wii·aa had made against the advent of a missionary.

"What have Iron Men brought to Haida Gwaii?" he asked. "The evil spirits of sickness. The evil spirits of firewater. Our fathers' eyes were like the eagles', " he reminded them.

"Now, everywhere, hunters' eyes are dimmed and their hands are weakened. Everywhere, lodges are empty." But they could work out their own salvation, he suggested, in their own way. "Remember that choice is the identifying symbol of the free man!" he urged. "And we are free men! We can choose to keep Iron Men out of Haida Gwaii."

Mr. Collison challenged that choice. Siigee's wife translated his Tsimshian speech into Haida:

"I came at Siigee's call," he pointed out reasonably. "Siigee's cry reached me. It came to me across the waves, and I have come to his call." His eyes searched the assembled throng. "And I will come again! When the first snow falls on the mountain tops, and the wildfowl are returning southward, I will come to stay!"

People argued, quietly and passionately.

"We can choose not to have him stay," some people reminded others. "Why should we let him stay? Those Tsimshian who follow the missionaries on the mainland have nothing now— no slaves, no handsome houses, no dances and feasts, no poles."

"But God doesn't like totem poles," the others contended in turn. "That's why we are being punished."

Young Siigee died that week, before the matter was settled.

"See!" medicine men gloated maliciously. "The Iron sorcerer could do nothing against his own sickness. He has no power."

People blackened their faces in mourning and wailed sadly for their lost sea hunter.

Chief 7idansuu paid glowing tribute to him.

"We could ill afford to lose young Siigee," he lamented to his family in private. "He had great influence with 7wii·aa."

Chief 7wii·aa was desolated by the loss of his young relative. "Siigee liked the missionary," he kept muttering to everybody. He moved like a broken man, while Siigee's widow hovered near him.

As the weeks went by, though, Chief 7wii·aa's old pride returned. "Choice is the identifying symbol of the free man," he quoted 7idansuu; and his tone made it a challenge to all Massett people. They, it suggested, could choose to defy the words of Chief 7idansuu if they thought he was mistaken. "Choice is the identifying symbol of the free man," he repeated often, and especially when he stood near his Kingii pole.

When Mr. Collison arrived with his family in October, Chief 7wii·aa gave him an abandoned fur storage hut to live in. He offered him the protection of membership in his Eagle family.

Mr. Collison graciously accepted Eagle membership, his wife and children thereby becoming Ravens. And he worked diligently with Siigee's widow to learn the difficult Haida language.

7idansuu showed no open disapproval. Massett was 7wii·aa's village. It belonged, too, to other families, who could choose to welcome a missionary—even though he thought the choice was unwise. Certainly he did not countenance the white man's presence by attending his first Christmas service.

"Christmas is dressup day," Siigee's widow informed the village. She knew, being from the mainland.

"Dressup day?" people echoed in dismay. How could they dress up to honor an occasion when they knew the missionary would not approve of their "heathen" dancing regalia?

A subchief had the answer. He had been to Victoria, and had bought out the wardrobe of an impoverished theatrical company. Now he went into business.

When Mr. Collison rang his bell on Christmas morning, he was astounded at the congregation that streamed into an abandoned feasthouse.

A subchief entered in an orange-and-green bathrobe; his wife was wrapped in a striped bedspread. A Raven prince followed as Harlequin, joyously a-jingle with bells. Then came an admiral without trousers, and a motley parade of half-naked generals and soldiers, and a chorus of befeathered ladies.

A really weird apparition entered next. A medicine man had bought himself a white surplice; and to relieve its plainness, he had wrapped his long, straggly hair around a pair of elk horns. His bony legs were bare.

Chief 7wii·aa arrived in his own magnificent sea otter cloak.

No Haida would fail in courtesy to any man's great occasion; this was a race with punctilious formal manners.

Fortunately, Mr. Collison and his family had good manners also.

"He's a man with a feeling heart," 7idansuu commented to Da·axiigang one day, a few months later.

They and he were at Fort Simpson with the year's canoes. And when they were ready to start back in patched trade-ins, the missionary asked if he might return to Haida Gwaii in the state canoe. Only two canoes looked seaworthy to him, he confessed: the chief's canoe and Da·axiigang's.

The latter had come to the fort to sell curios and not canoes. His smaller craft was sound, but filled. He had his new wife with him, the younger princess who was now eighteen, and their attendants. He had chests full of eulachon oil, Hudson's Bay blankets, and mountain goat horns. He also had a new gun.

Chief 7idansuu installed Mr. Collison in the seventy-two-foot canoe and started homeward with thirty other Massett and ₭ung canoes. As usual, the fleet coasted northwestward along the Alaskan islands; from a certain camp site at Cape Chacon, they could watch the weather for a forty-mile dash straight south across the sea to Massett.

En route to Chacon, they decided to call on Chief Kinnanook at Tongas. He and 7idansuu were cultivating friendly relations these days, having agreed that their people could no longer afford to decimate one another. Too, Mr. Collison had been invited to visit Tongas, once, when he had removed three bullets from Chief Kinnanook's body.

The Haida arrived at Tongas on a Saturday. They were well received, though Chief Kinnanook was not at home. And they agreed to stay briefly for a visit.

Mr. Collison took the opportunity of holding a Sunday service. He preached in Tsimshian, and also in Chinook.

"I'm always a little nervous about speaking in Chinook," he

admitted to Chief 7idansuu. One missionary whom Mr. Collison knew had meant to address some native people as "children of the forest"; but, in the always inadequate trade jargon, it had come out as "little men stationed among the sticks," with unhappy consequences.

7idansuu enjoyed this joke immensely. He rather liked the missionary. "We'll have to stay here for several days," he cautioned Mr. Collison, after studying the sky to the north.

"Then I would like to make a quick visit to Metlakatla," Mr. Collison said wistfully. "We haven't come far north of the fort, have we? And Metlakatla's not far south of it."

Metlakatla had been the ancient winter home of many Tsimshian people, abandoned when they moved to cluster around their relative's cannons at the fort. Now it had been reactivated. It had become the isolated haven for Tsimshian Christians under the aggressive leadership of an Episcopalian missionary, Mr. Duncan. "I would like to see how they're getting on," Mr. Collison explained, "and I believe Rear Admiral Prevost was to visit Mr. Duncan this week."

Prevost—both 7idansuu and Gu·uu recalled the name. Prevost was the King George man who had come to Haida Gwaii after the *Susan Sturgis* affair. He had given Gu·uu a *Book*.

"I remember him," Gu·uu said now, "and I'd like to see him again."

"I would, too," said Chief 7idansuu. "Mr. Collison, since Chief Kinnanook isn't here, I'll take you myself." He looked a little uneasily about him, however. Something was astir in Tongas. He shrugged off his concern. "Just ancient enmity," he told himself. "Still, I think you'd better stay here, Da·axiigang, and keep an eye on things," he said to his nephew.

He left quickly, to be back quickly, traveling by the pale light of a northern summer night.

As he had sensed, there was something astir at Tongas. A

143

deserter from one of the United States Alaskan garrisons had taught the villagers how to make *hoochinoo,* firewater, from molasses, potatoes, and berries. Their "still" consisted of coal oil cans and "worms" of long, hollow kelp tubes.

As soon as the chief and the missionary had disappeared into the pale glow, Massett and Ḵung families were invited to an informal feast. And *hoochinoo* was served at the feast.

Da·aχiigang did not go to the feast, preferring a restful visit to a Tongas carver with a fellow-carver, a Massett subchief. And it was very late at night when they were disturbed by the hullabaloo from the feasthouse.

They rushed in to investigate. "It's like Raven's curse," Da·aχ iigang muttered, glaring at intoxicated men, women, and children. "Why did you do this to my people?" he demanded of the presiding host, Kinnanook's father. The Massett subchief did not ask. He grabbed a small, carved seat and hurled it at the old man.

Pandemonium broke loose.

Ḵung and Massett men who had refused to drink *hoochinoo* now leapt up to support their leaders. "Get out! Get out!" they ordered staggering people. And they helped Da·aχiigang whisk the furious Massett subchief out of the feasthouse before a Tongas could kill him.

"Keep him out of sight!" Da·aχiigang ordered. He himself rushed to his chests to bring back fifty Hudson's Bay blankets and his new gun to offer to the affronted father of Chief Kinnanook. He laid his peace offering at the old man's feet with respectful formality, but his eyes were glittering with anger. He dashed back to the beach. "We must get away," he urged. "You know the chief is trying to restore peace between us and Kinnanook's people."

Canoe-men glanced anxiously at the sky to the north, then even more anxiously back at the feasthouse from which yelling men were emerging with torches. The sea was the lesser danger.

Before the brief Alaskan night had ended, they launched Massett and Ƙung canoes and headed into the threatening north. Drunk men, women, and children sprawled among the chests; sober men, women, and children paddled and bailed.

Da·aᶍiigang's chieftainess paddled as grimly as the others. She remembered another venture out into wild waters, the flight from Jalun River at the time of the epidemic.

"We'll try to make Chacon," Da·aᶍiigang said as they rushed onward through a red dawn. If the Tongas followed, however, he knew they might have to attempt the crossing to Massett in the patched-up canoes.

———

Entering Metlakatla Pass that same morning, Chief 7idansuu was sad. When he had come here as a boy, nine handsome villages had nestled along the meandering channel. Now there was only the stark town where Mr. Duncan ruled his thousand converts.

"It's so bleak!" the chief said, dismayed by the long, straight row of ugly, unpainted, two-storey houses made of whipsawed lumber. There were no projecting, carved beams to relieve the plainness, no colorful totem poles standing against the forest.

A few flags were whipping out in honor of a visitor, Rear Admiral Prevost, retired. People wore their Sunday clothes, and their Sabbath manners.

"They look so awkward in those clothes," 7idansuu remarked to his son. He longed for the beauty of muscles rippling under wet skin; he sighed for the flash of bracelets and anklets on now soberly garbed women.

People answered to strange foreign names like George and

Henry. Brash young commoners snapped out orders to men who had been chiefs. And no one danced in welcome, or wafted the eagle-down of peace and friendship. "It's so bleak without the old ways and the old totems," he protested to Gu·uu.

"But nobody died at Metlakatla," Gu·uu pointed out; and his tone surprised his father.

Mr. Duncan and his converts had moved to Metlakatla in May 1862, just before the terrible smallpox summer. Their deliberate isolation from the "heathen" had saved them from infection.

"There were no totem poles here," Gu·uu continued, "and people didn't die here."

At Metlakatla, poles had been burned with righteous enthusiasm.

Mr. Collison came up to them at that moment. "Just see the vegetable gardens!" he said.

There was a neat little garden in front of each ugly house. There were precise picket fences to keep out playing children and dogs.

7idansuu glanced at them coldly. For some reason he could never quite fathom, white men thought that great virtue lay in gardens. To dig the soil seemed to be a superior thing to do; though the Power-of-the-Shining-Heavens had clearly ordained this as a land of rock, forest, moss, and sea; and had bountifully provided for the people with sea foods and fruits. Why should it be so worthy to dig a garden? True, the Haida grew potatoes and valued them. But why should they be tied to gardens when there were clams to dig and salmon to catch and seaweed and berries to gather? What was so good about gardens?

He was genuinely impressed by the blacksmith shop, astounded by the sawmill and bakery. But he concealed his disapproval of the town's weaving industry, except from Gu·uu.

"Why don't they weave beauty into their blankets?" he said to his son as he fingered shoddy woolen cloth. "Why don't they design them with patterns, like the Chilkat?" Surely any native person knew that Chilkat blankets were greatly increased in value by the beauty of their pattern, an intricate pattern of flattened ovals.

"God doesn't like totem patterns," Gu·uu answered. A glint of defiance brightened his eyes.

7idansuu turned a startled look on his son. "Handsome blankets would sell better," he retorted. But maybe they wouldn't now, he thought, recalling the ugly plainness of spoons, dishes, storage boxes, and even canoes in this model Christian village. God did not like totem poles. Apparently He did not like decoration in any form.

He could see that Admiral Prevost considered Metlakatla vastly superior to any native village. But what a white man thought was unimportant to 7idansuu. It was Gu·uu's thoughts that perturbed him, and the way Gu·uu sailed in the wake of the missionaries.

He was thankful to leave the depressing village early Tuesday morning. The night had been wild; and though the storm had blown over, the sky was still threatening. Still, they would be hugging the shore, and he was uneasy about Tongas, so they set out.

Actually, sailing conditions proved excellent. They reached Tongas at noon, just as the wind was freshening again into a squall.

"Where are the canoes?" the chief said, alarmed.

His entire fleet had vanished.

"I'll investigate this," Mr. Collison announced, with a white man's assumption of command.

It was appreciation of an old situation, not a new meekness, that made 7idansuu acquiesce. He put the missionary ashore.

Then he hovered, ready to fight or to run as the moment dictated.

Mr. Collison strode to the biggest house. Chief Kinnanook had not returned, but his sister told the missionary of the terrible affront to her father. A Massett subchief had hurled a seat at him.

"It's your own fault," Mr. Collison retorted, turning his angry face towards the old man. He was furious about the *hoochinoo;* and his fury was not fettered by the diplomatic niceties of intertribal behavior. Fired by righteous indignation, he tongue-lashed even Kinnanook's sister and father for serving firewater to Haida families.

"You speak the truth," the chieftainess admitted. "And I'm glad my brother wasn't here to avenge the affront. Tell Chief 7idansuu I beg him to leave at once for Haida Gwaii. Our peoples must not decimate one another any further."

Chief 7idansuu left in fury. Those treacherous Tongas! Because of them, his people had ventured north into a storm in patched-up canoes while many of them were possessed by evil spirits of firewater! Da·aхiigang, he thought, and fear clutched at his heart. His heir's health was not equal to too great a strain.

Swiftly, the seventy-two-foot canoe coasted northward and westward along the Alaskan islands, climbing white crests and plunging into awful green caverns.

As they neared Chacon, the wind slacked off.

"Da·aхiigang!" The chief sagged with relief.

Da·aхiigang's canoe had nosed stealthily out of a cove to investigate, and his face had been blackened for war. He had been ready to fight the Tongas, and to fight them at sea as the Haida had always fought them.

Now, seeing it was his uncle, Da·aхiigang shouted joyously to his fleet. Canoes shot into view. They escorted 7idansuu into camp. And the minute the canoes were beached, even the head chief of the Sdast'a·aas Eagles joined a frantically capering circle; his shouts rose as wildly as anyone else's.

After this volcanic expression of relief, however, those who had drunk *hoochinoo* stood shamed before the chief.

"Do you want to be slaves of gluttony?" he asked them. "Or do you want to stay free men?"

———

The fleet was weather-bound at Chacon for two whole weeks. At last, one morning, the weather appeared settled. They started across the ocean. Halfway to Massett, a sou'westerly squall struck them, right out of the wide Pacific. Rain slashed them. Huge waves, crested with foam, broke around them, threatening to swamp the canoes.

7idansuu steered the seventy-two-foot canoe, holding her handsome prow into the seas.

Mr. Collison prayed, and bailed.

Gu·uu struggled with oil chests that broke loose from fastenings. A lid was wrenched off an oil chest; oil splashed out, and the hungry sea licked it, and grew smooth near the big canoe.

"If we could only see!" people groaned. With the wind snatching spray from the crest of every gigantic wave, they could see only a few yards around them. They peered anxiously, but futilely, for some sight of relatives' canoes. They strained their ears for some sound of the spit. Rose Spit was always waiting with its dread storm spirits and sea monsters.

Suddenly the squall lifted.

"There are the canoes!" people shouted.

"We're on course!" they cried.

Relatives came rushing forth from Massett to help them.

"Not one person was lost!" Chief 7idansuu marveled. "Every

patched canoe rode out the storm!"

"He who calmed the angry waves of the Galilean Sea was with us," Mr. Collison asserted.

It was Gu·uu, not his father, who translated that message. And his eyes shone with a strange excitement. As soon as he reached Ƙung, he took out the New Testament the officer had once given him. "I wonder what it says," he kept remarking as he rifled its ghost leaves.

"Gu·uu is restless," 7idansuu observed.

"Everyone's restless here," Da·aẍiigang countered. "The people are not happy at Ƙung."

"It's time to leave Ƙung to the ghosts," Chief 7idansuu announced. The people could not bear to live there any longer.

"Ƙung is so far away from everyone else," they agreed, though they had never before thought of their home as remote. It would be good to move northwest along the shore, they said, closer to other people.

——————————— N I N E ———————————

"WE'LL BE HAPPY AT YATZ," Ḵung families assured one another as they traveled to Tow Hill the following spring to dig razor clams, and also to grub among the spruces for the long roots they would later roast over a fire to loosen the bark, then split and weave into waterproof canoe hats.

Da·aẍiigang's lovely young chieftainess was an artist at weaving canoe hats. And her husband delighted in decorating them with stunning, painted crests. A hat from their hands brought a gold piece from collectors. Then Da·aẍiigang hammered the gold piece into a bracelet that sold as readily as the hat.

People caught the young couple's enthusiasm for old Haida skills, 7idansuu noticed. He was sure the people would settle down happily with them at Yatz.

Meanwhile, it was delightful at Tow Hill, with blue sea and white breakers and sand dunes and sea grasses. Hard-packed sand curved away to Rose Spit, shimmering here and there with fresh-water seepage and with mirages. Every spanking breeze carried either the iodine tang of the sea or else the honeyed scent of opening cottonwood buds from along the river.

Then the ground turned blue with violets; lacy mosses were embroidered with perfumed pink moccasin flowers; and among the open, wide-spreading spruce trees, blue grouse puffed themselves with pride as they drummed for their ladies.

"We'll be happy at Yatz," the chief said wistfully to his nephew. "We'll build handsome new houses." He sighed before he added, "Gu·uu will like it at Yatz."

Gu·uu had not come with them to Tow Hill. Nor had he gone west to fish with the other group of families. Nor had he gone to Kaigani where he truly belonged now that he was a man.

Gu·uu had gone to Massett. With his New Testament!

"What does it say, Mr. Collison?" Gu·uu asked, opening his book to the flyleaf where the naval officer had written something.

The missionary read it to him: "To the Indian Boy, Edensaw's son. I trust that the bread cast upon the waters will soon be found.—James C. Prevost, Captain, HMS *Satellite*."

He explained what the words meant. "Why, this is the word from the Chief Above, Gu·uu!" he exclaimed.

"Yes," Gu·uu agreed reverently. "It's a sign, Mr. Collison." He gazed skyward, then back at the missionary. He spoke in strangely excited tones. "That's what it said all this time and

I never knew it. It's a sign! It's a sign from the God who does not like totem poles. A sign to me!" He had the look of a Haida boy seeing his spirit vision. And from that moment, he became Mr. Collison's most ardent pupil.

———————————

Because Gu·uu was a very high-ranking Raven and the son of one of the highest-ranking Haida Eagles, his influence was tremendous. If Gu·uu wanted to learn to read, all the young men wanted to learn to read.

Classes swelled at Massett.

Chief 7wii·aa's pride swelled with the classes. He would gain prestige from villagers who could read, he knew. And his Ḵingii pole, the symbol of survival, would gain power from the fact that 7idansuu's own son was sheltering behind it.

7idansuu had a younger son now, Sun-Lak-Kwee-Kun's child, who was a Kaigani Raven like his mother, and like Gu·uu.

"What about your Kaigani Ravens?" Chief 7idansuu demanded of his older son later that year. "What about helping your uncles make their stand against *hoochinoo* in Alaska?"

"I'll have more power to help them when Mr. Collison puts the *sign* on me," Gu·uu assured him with almost mystic fervor.

"By that time you won't care about your duty," his father charged.

For just a moment there was the old delightful glint of fun in Gu·uu's eyes. "Choice is the identifying symbol of the free man," he mischievously quoted his accuser; but before he had finished the quote, the impudent glint was gone. There was only the intensity of the Christian convert.

"He'll become like the men at Metlakatla," 7idansuu predicted with as much anger as sorrow. Something like panic gripped him. His own dearly loved son was going to shirk his responsibilities; he was going to be called George or Henry and be commanded by commoners; he was going to renounce his just debts.

Chief 7idansuu believed that a hereditary chief had a responsibility to remain a hereditary chief. He was born to the responsibility and trained for it. A chief knew Haida law, and he knew how to maintain it. He saw that he and his people returned to another chief and his people the wealth, even more than the wealth, they had received. He cherished the potlatch.

The potlatch approved and recorded claims. It saw every debt paid. It stimulated trade, family feeling, decoration, dancing, and storytelling. Yet missionaries condemned it. They called the feasthouse arts a waste of time. Their bleak converts hid behind righteousness, he had noticed, while they repudiated their just debts along with their heritage of culture, while they cheated their creditors out of the very blankets those creditors were counting on to pay their own just debts.

"If I couldn't pay my debts in public, the disgrace would be more than I could bear," 7idansuu stormed to his family. "There'll be a potlatch for the house-raising at Yatz!" he promised. "And what a potlatch!" People were going to gasp at the carving on the house poles. They were going to be overwhelmed by the beauty of the ceremonies.

He leapt into preparations. He carved as he had not been free to carve since youth, and he fairly glowed as he carved. His villagers caught his spirit. Pride in their heritage began to stir like life in a seed.

As though to confirm this resurgence of life, that year a boy was born in Skidegate, the boy who was Da·axiigang's heir by the rules of succession.

"Da·axiigang's heir!" the chief whispered happily as he carved.

He frowned when the child was taken to Victoria to live with his white father. "White men!" he muttered furiously.

He was even more infuriated by white men that autumn of 1877, when he visited Massett. He came home livid.

"Maybe Iron Men don't need the potlatch," he burst out to his family. "They don't have to record things by public witness; they can put things down on papers. Papers!" He almost spat the word.

At Massett, a fine old Eagle had been dying; and he had presented his head chief with his most prized possession, a testimonial from a white man he had once helped. It was a paper he had taken pride in displaying.

"What does it say?" 7idansuu had asked Mr. Collison. He had long entertained suspicions about that paper.

The missionary had read it:

"To Whom It May Concern: The bearer of this paper is a dirty old savage and a bum."

"It was meant as a joke," Mr. Collison had placatingly explained, although he flushed. "Some white man thought it would amuse other white men."

Recalling the incident for Da·axiigang, 7idansuu was angry all over again. For a cheap guffaw, a white man had stripped a fine old Haida of his dignity. "Perhaps it's well that Gu·uu learns to read," he went on. Then a thought struck him silent. Now, any chief needed this Iron skill to protect his people from humiliation as well as from injustice. But to acquire the skill, he had to submit, like a child, to being taught by a foreigner, by a member of an inferior race.

In the important ways, Iron Men were inferior, he contended. They were not trustworthy. They had bad manners. They lacked a sense of justice. They lacked sensitivity. They didn't even hear and see as well as a native person, nor move as gracefully. A chief must make a stand against them, he said; he must sway his people for their own good.

He grabbed an adze and went ferociously to work on a house post. A chief's stand could harm his people. Iron Men had guns to shatter a village. They had papers to prove outrageous claims. Worst of all, they had God.

If only a missionary had not come to Haida Gwaii, he thought. Missionaries were such aggressive men. They were so absolutely sure they were absolutely right that they convinced a wavering, anxious, uncertain people. They didn't give true convictions time to grow.

"Our only reliable support comes from the medicine men," he said ruefully to his heir. "And they work more from spite and vanity than from concern for the welfare of the people."

———————

Much more violently than Chief 7idansuu, the Massett medicine men resented the missionary. Both his God and his medical techniques were a threat to their own influence in the village. He defied the very source of their strength, the occult power that worked through them.

Even though they used all the sorcery they possessed, they repeatedly failed to kill him. Mr. Collison simply did not die— as a native person would have died—when the medicine men put hairs from his head into their deathboxes. Also, Mr. Collison dared to cure patients they had pronounced as beyond hope.

"You have shamed us before our people," their delegation said to him one day, "and we must have payment from you for this or we shall wash off our shame with your blood."

Mr. Collison did not pay them. He thundered at them. "The great Chief of Heaven forbids you to continue your wicked witchcraft over the sick!"

One doctor was wily. "Put the sign of the Chief of Heaven on me," he suggested. "It will give me new power with the people and I won't need to wipe out my shame with your blood."

The missionary indignantly explained that a good-medicine label pasted onto a bottle of poison would not transform that poison into good medicine. It would still kill the patient. And he continued to wage unrelenting war on witchcraft.

"He's so aggressive," 7idansuu protested to Da·axiigang. "He's in such a terrible hurry! He's making the people deceitful."

People were becoming deceitful at Massett. Mindful that this man's God was indeed wiping out the villages, they grew more and more secretive about the practices he condemned. Yet they actually pursued those practices more avidly than ever. Witchcraft, gambling, and *hoochinoo* offered escape from a deep and dreadful bafflement.

"The missionary only adds to their shame and confusion," 7idansuu raged. Then he leapt into work again. He would lift shame and confusion by reminding people that renewal was the law of life. It was good to be working hard as a carver again, he found. He went out with the seal hunters; and it was good to be out sea hunting. He found renewal himself in doing what the Haida had always done, in filling and enriching the blank areas of both time and space.

His villagers caught his spirit. The law of life began working in them, as well. "What a house-raising potlatch this will be!" they said to one another. They were busy, and happy, except when disturbing news came from Massett.

In Massett, one of the most respected of the house chiefs now fell from grace, as the Raven had fallen. Eagle Chief Sdiihldaa, a sea hunter, became a slave to his own craving for the liquor he distilled from berries and potatoes and from Hudson's Bay Company molasses.

He became desperately ill that autumn of 1877. And as he

lay dying in his gigantic cedar house, the missionary's prayers competed with the medicine men's drums and rattles.

The medicine men said Sdiihldaa's illness was caused by an evil spirit in one of his slaves. They kept torturing this slave with pitch-pine torches to drive out the evil spirit which, they claimed, had assumed the form of a mouse. If the chief died, this slave was to be shot by another slave who stood ready with a musket.

Chief Sdiihldaa died.

Mr. Collison leapt into battle.

At his signal, Chief 7wii·aa and young Gu·uu grabbed the slave with the musket; they freed the slave with the supposed evil spirit.

"You all heard Chief Sdiihldaa's words," the missionary reminded the startled people. "You heard him say that had he lived, he would have been first in the way of the Chief Above."

The people had indeed heard remorseful Sdiihldaa say this. And now they read fervent purpose in the faces of their own Town Chief 7wii·aa and Gu·uu; a mighty Eagle and a famous Raven. So they fell back in dismay while the missionary laid out their chief for Christian burial.

True, they wailed and blackened their faces; they danced the death dance around the dead chief for three days, reverently scattering swan's-down and eagle-down on his body. But they did not prevent the missionary and his supporters from burying Sdiihldaa in the ground. God did not like the smell of the corpses in the mortuary poles. And they didn't want any more punishment from Him.

In retaliation for the affront, the medicine men launched a whisper campaign. "Iron Men have promised to pay Mr. Collison many blankets and gold pieces for every Haida he can bury in the ground," they whispered around the village. "He will never stop until he has buried every Haida in the ground. None of you will be safe from him."

This thought alarmed the people. It could be true. It could well be part of God's plan for wiping out the villages, and also part of Mr. Collison's plan for being wealthy, as all men wanted to be.

In the midst of the confusion, a dangerously bitter dispute arose over the ownership of Sdiihldaa's slaves. And during a drunken rage, a handsome young subchief injured his wife. When she died, he tried to kill himself from grief and horror.

Mr. Collison took the occasion to drive home a truth. "If it were true that I wanted to bury all the Haida, would I oppose the *hoochinoo* that kills so many of you?" he asked reasonably.

This, too, was whispered around the village. People saw the truth in it. So they listened respectfully to Mr. Collison when he offered to arbitrate the dispute about Sdiihldaa's slaves. They saw that Town Chief 7wii·aa and Gu·uu supported the arbitration.

Chief 7idansuu came to Massett when he heard of the trouble. He talked to Gu·uu.

He also listened to Gu·uu. "Do you want bloodshed?" his son challenged him.

7idansuu did not want bloodshed. Nor did he want a further undermining of the authority of the chiefs in any village. Obviously this was not the moment to make a stand. Patience and the law of life always prevailed, he knew. They would prevail again. Concealing his reluctance, he added his support to arbitration. He attended the subsequent dance of peace in Big House.

"Mr. Collison is town chief of Massett now," he told Da·a ̱xiigang when he reached home.

"At least he's an Eagle," his nephew observed. Da·a ̱xiigang was in high spirits. He had just finished polishing an exceptionally successful slate totem pole, a twenty-five-inch illustration of "The Raven Steals the Sun." "My heart feels good," he said as he turned the argillite column to let its contours catch the light.

7idansuu laid a fond hand on the sculptor's shoulder. He examined his work with delight. Yet he could not shake off his concern. "As soon as Mr. Collison's strong enough, he'll free the slaves at Massett," he predicted. "He'll outlaw the potlatch. No one will own anything."

"But who can stop the wind?" his nephew asked him gently. "Who can turn back a river?"

"Mr. Collison's not quite the wind," his uncle retorted, "nor is he a river. A time will come to stop him." A white man might be ruthlessly aggressive; but a Haida was as ruthlessly patient.

───

Chief 7idansuu was still waiting for his time, however, when spring sent him seal hunting; and when he returned, it was to find Dr. Dawson waiting for him.

Dr. Dawson had been charged with charting the coastline of the Queen Charlotte Islands for the Geological Survey of Canada, and with reporting in detail on the villages and their people. He asked the assistance of this important chief.

7idansuu was pleased to serve as pilot on the *Wanderer*. It was well for a chief to know the Iron Men as thoroughly as possible. And this Iron Man, he swiftly discovered, was of a superior nation. He wasn't greedy like the traders. He wasn't rushing to change everything, like the missionaries. He was more like a native person; he had time and patience to look and to listen. He didn't arrive knowing everything; he came to learn something, to learn something from a native person.

For his part, Dr. Dawson found 7idansuu of a superior

nation, too. He was repeatedly astounded by his pilot's inti-mate knowledge of every reef, cove, current, and tide rip around Haida Gwaii. And the chief knew every village, every custom and legend; he knew where every bird nested, where every fish swam, and where every devilfish might be lurking. He read the sky like a book, the sea like a marine chart. His knowledge was truly stupendous.

During that wet, stormy summer, they found the forest weep-ing over many a village it was reclaiming. Sometimes they found two or three people occupying a vast house that was moulder-ing away around them. At Koyah's village, there was only deso-lation.

"But why would a tribe abandon a splendid village like K'yuusdaa?" Dr. Dawson asked when they got there. Myth House still looked inviting. Sea Lion House was handsome. The heraldic column of Pole-Reaching-the-Sky House stood straight as a living cedar, though other houses were succumb-ing sadly.

Chief 7idansuu did not tell him why people would aban-don a splendid village like this. It was a Haida reason.

When the 1878 trip was over, Dr. Dawson published a report that tended to confirm what travelers had long been claiming, that the Haida were perhaps the finest looking and most highly cultured of the North American Indians.

"But the authority of the chiefs is now very small," the report stated. It was even smaller over on the mainland, Dr. Dawson indicated. "At Fort Simpson," he said, "most of the totem poles have been cut down through missionary influence." He did not add that the unique totem poles of the Pacific northwest were actually being chopped up for firewood in misdirected zeal.

Dr. Dawson's report alarmed scholars all over the Western world. The most accomplished artists of the North American Indians were dying out fast; their unique society was dying out even faster; a truly extraordinary culture was vanishing from the earth, practically unrecorded.

Museum curators and art collectors were as alarmed as the anthropologists and ethnologists. Every day, they knew, totem poles were being ruthlessly burned up. Every day, Haida artists who produced the exquisite slate sculptures were either dying or else turning shamed backs on their heritage. Already it might be too late to save much!

James Swan hurried to the Queen Charlotte Islands to pick up argillite pieces for the Philadelphia Centennial Exhibition. The Smithsonian Institution sent him back again for "caskets, plaques, columns, and curios elaborately and elegantly carved in high relief." James Deans was dispatched to gather exhibits for the World's Columbian Exposition at Chicago. The British Association for the Advancement of Science sent in Professor Franz Boas, an anthropologist fascinated with primitive art. Dr. Charles Newcombe of Victoria began collecting for Ottawa, Washington, and New York. Museums appealed to Da·axiigang for models of Haida houses and totem poles and canoes, and for sketches illustrating customs, and for the tales and traditions that went with the models and the sketches.

Chief 7idansuu's none too robust heir found himself swamped with art commissions, inundated with scholarly visits.

But that was later. That was after the publication of Dr. Dawson's report on the Queen Charlotte Islands.

———

That same year, the people of Ḵung were able to leave their village to its ghosts. Then they paddled away in silence.

Forlorn carved and painted figures found lonely voices in the ravens who cried from housetops and totem poles. Seagulls screamed, too; and eagles shrieked from the sky.

The villagers paddled north and west, in the direction of K'yuusdaa, nearly halfway to the Jalun River, where the princesses had been snatched to safety. And here, at Yatz, they made their home.

"It's better here for starting on trips to Kaigani and Fort Simpson," they told one another. Nobody mentioned Victoria.

At the same time, 7idansuu was defending the embattled culture. He was working tirelessly to entrench it at Yatz. And in his Haida way, he was patiently waiting for the right moment to stand up to the missionary.

What could he do, under threat of gunboats that could, and would, shell a village? What could he do against the power of God's missionary? What should he do for the real welfare of the people?

Mr. Collison was not plagued by such doubts. He knew what he should do. He acted with conviction. He should stamp out heathen ways and heathen symbols. Especially he should stamp out slavery and the potlatch. The potlatch was a ruinous waste of time, time that could usefully have been employed for work.

Soon after Dr. Dawson's departure from the islands, Mr. Collison heard of an outbreak of smallpox among distant Alaskan nations. At once he secured a supply of vaccine lymph from the newly organized Indian Department of the Canadian government. He called Massett people to a meeting.

The villagers trembled to think of another epidemic. Yet they shrank away from the vaccine, even after the missionary vaccinated himself before their eyes. It was when he was actually striding from the building in wrath that a subchief leapt to his feet. "Chief!" the young man called. "Put the mark on me, too!"

Others followed his lead. Then nearly all the villagers decided to acquire the mystic mark that would give them protection from the evil spirits of Kali Koustli.

In a very few days, they began to fall sick. Arms, shoulders, and necks swelled; flesh flamed; fevers mounted.

Medicine men watched with glittering eyes. "He will bury all of you," they gloated.

Panic spread through the village. Town Chief 7wii·aa and Gu·uu kept angry men from shooting Mr. Collison as he and his wife worked to allay swellings and fevers.

"Tattoos swell up and grow red," Gu·uu reminded fellow sufferers, "yet you are ashamed to let a groan escape you then."

The medicine men waited.

But people began to get well; and it was their turn to gloat. They could scoff at the medicine men, now. They could scoff even at Kali Koustli, now. His evil spirits could never hurt them again.

It was a great victory!

Word of the vaccine spread. Families rushed into Massett from other villages to let Mr. Collison put the magic mark on them, too. Some even followed Gu·uu and Town Chief 7wii·aa into baptism to win the supreme sign of power, the Cross.

7idansuu's son was the first official convert. He was registered as "George Cowhoe."

"The Kaigani Ravens have lost Gu·uu," the chief said sadly. Yet how could he protest in good conscience? Governor Douglas had once explained about vaccination to him.

At Massett, there was a surge of enthusiasm for the missionary. He had overcome the most dreaded of all evil spirits, the spirits of Kali Koustli. He had overcome them with power he received from the God who had proved he could devastate everybody. "Maybe God won't wipe out any more villages if we follow him," people said, streaming in to hear the Gospel.

Even the medicine men conceded defeat. The power of God's

sorcerer was manifestly greater than their own. A few of them were baptized, relinquishing charms and rattles. Later, though, they begged to have the charms and rattles returned. Their affronted spirits wouldn't leave them in peace, they explained to the missionary.

When Chief 7idansuu arrived at Massett that year for a minor potlatch, no blackened slaves rushed into the surf to cast coppers under his canoe. No dancers moved on the beach, wafting feathers. Instead, a choir of young people in European clothing sang hymns.

But they would see the beauty of the old ways when they came to the Yatz potlatch, 7idansuu promised himself; they would return to the native wisdoms. And he went back to his preparations with purposeful vigor. The house-raising at Yatz would start a great resurgence of Haida ways!

He was not informed of further changes even then impending at Massett. No white man needed native sanction for changes he knew to be good for native people.

———

Mr. Offutt, a Sacramento man with a native Indian family and a native way of life, had managed a tiny post for the Hudson's Bay Company for years, operating in a log hut on a hill behind the village. Now this trader was retiring.

"This is the chance to make a real change here," Mr. Collison said to his wife. "The Company will be sending in a new man. Why shouldn't he be Commissioner of the Peace, as well as trader? I think Massett is ready now for good British law and order." There would be no more slavery, he knew, once British law was enforced. Even American slaves had always found freedom under the Union Jack.

His zeal for a visible freedom may have blinded him to a

subtler issue of freedom, a people's right to self-determination. Perhaps he overlooked the fact that choice is the identifying symbol of the free man.

He wrote to the attorney general.

And in 1879, Mr. Alexander McKenzie arrived as Hudson's Bay trader and Commissioner of the Peace at Massett. In future, all disputes and claims would be settled by him. Gunboats would be called to enforce his decisions. "But how in the name of the world am I going to maintain peace among the pirates of the Pacific?" he implored Mr. Collison in private.

"They're no longer pirates," the missionary assured him with considerable satisfaction. And he advised Mr. McKenzie to swear in four high-ranking converts as peace officers. All four stood over six feet; all four had the confident bearing of the high born; all four could command obedience from the villagers.

The first officer sworn in to maintain British justice on the Queen Charlotte Islands was 7idansuu's own son, "George Cowhoe." The second was the new young Chief Sdiihldaa.

To impress these four young men with the majesty of their queen, and of her empire, Mr. Collison showed them a world map with the empire "on which the sun never sets" painted out in red. "And this is Haida Gwaii," he told them proudly, pointing to the Queen Charlotte Islands, also painted red.

"You are lying to me," Gu·uu charged. He glared at the insignificance of the islands lying off the great mainland of North America.

His fellow officers were fully as indignant. That little thing? Haida Gwaii! It was an insult not to be tolerated. All four stalked angrily out of court.

They forgot their anger, however, when they learned that Mr. Collison was leaving them almost immediately to serve his church on the mainland. They organized a great sendoff for him: Union Jacks and Stars and Stripes flew from housetops;

a cannon saluted from the front of Big House; all the house chiefs of Massett escorted the missionary out to his steamer. Everyone sang hymns.

Chief 7idansuu and Da·axiigang were not there to see him go. They were at Yatz, adding the final touch to decorations that were going to win back the people.

But the chief was not happy. "The queen has sent her law to Haida Gwaii," he fumed, "and it's my own fault. I should have known she would be offended and retaliate against us." He rubbed a carving in angry silence. "At least we're rid of that missionary," he burst out.

They raised the house at Yatz, and people exclaimed at its beauty. Yet they were visibly ill at ease over the carved poles, the ceremonies, the "heathen" dancing, the ancient stories. 7idansuu's heart ached more and more as the potlatch progressed. It was going to take more time than he had realized to bring people back to the native wisdoms.

Shortly after the potlatch, a message came from Victoria; and almost immediately the chief and his family went south by the Inside Passage.

They brought a boy, Da·axiigang's heir, back with them. "His white father wanted to take him to England," Sun-Lak-Kwee-Kun told people. "We had to steal him away."

"Hmph!" people said in Skidegate and Massett. "A very likely story! No doubt the white father deserted, the way white men do."

If that was the humiliating truth, Saang gaahl Eagles and Kaigani Ravens did not betray it by the flick of an eyelash. They had had to steal Da·axiigang's heir away from his white father, they said, or they would have lost the precious young prince. He would have gone to England.

They had scarcely settled the boy in when the next big change rocked them.

In 1884, the Potlatch Law was enacted.

"You mean that a man could go to jail for half a year for giving or attending a potlatch?" Chief 7idansuu demanded when he was informed of the Potlatch Law by the Commissioner of the Peace at Massett. "Then how do we pay our debts now?"

"The way white men pay debts, Chief."

"White men! Why must you always try to make us like white men? Why must your ways always be right? Why must everything that sustained our ancestors be evil?" He stood in anger for a minute. Then he drew himself up, a truly commanding figure. "I shall pay my debts as I have always paid them, in public and with ceremony. I shall conduct our affairs as I have always conducted them, in public and with ceremony. And try to put me in jail! Try to put my people in jail!" He strode from the courtroom.

For a week he sat in silence at home. "Why must all our ways be evil?" he implored Da·aхiigang one evening.

"We know they're not evil."

"Do we?" the chief challenged. "Do we? After Kwanduhadgaa's vision, are even you and I absolutely certain that totem poles are not evil?"

Da·aхiigang wanted to shout yes! "I suppose they could be evil," he reluctantly admitted. Then instantly he added, "But you don't believe it. I don't believe it. And chiefs have a duty—"

The chief raised a hand for silence. "Chiefs have a duty," he agreed. "The welfare of their people. Have you and I been able to make ours happy? Would we make them any happier by breaking the queen's law and bringing gunboats to shell the village? Da·aхiigang, who stands to lose most if we honor the Potlatch Law?"

"You and I. But we could—"

"The old days are dead," 7idansuu was saying. "The old days when people had faith in the spirits all around them; when they could always find help from their own guardian spirit. Now they feel lost and alone. But maybe, like Gu·uu, they could find a new power to help them, Da·axiigang. People must have a power beyond their own human power."

"Our people must have more than power," Da·axiigang replied with spirit. He scowled at his own thoughts. "Ours must have prestige. They must be lords of the coast. Right now they crave the prestige of leading in the new Iron skills, almost useless skills like reading!"

He thought of the young people.

"When are we going to learn to read papers?" the young people at Yatz kept asking. "When are we going to have a brass band?"

The Tsimshian, they said, the Tsimshian, were actually teaching reading in villages on the mainland. The Tsimshian at Metlakatla had a fine big brass band.

"We're falling behind," they complained. "And the Haida always used to be first."

As if reading his nephew's thoughts about the restlessness of the young people, 7idansuu spoke out. "I will not put my people into worse confusion. There are too many escapes from confusion. Too many evil escapes. Da·axiigang, a chief must give strength to his people. Now, there's only one way I can give strength to mine. I am going to stand with Gu·uu and young Sdiihldaa."

Da·axiigang gasped with surprise. Then he looked deeply into his uncle's eyes. "Where you stand, I stand," he said. And he turned away quickly. He couldn't bear to see the anguish in his beloved uncle's face.

"Uncle," he said gently, "I remember things you said to me

when you were teaching me to design—the things you said your uncle had taught you."

Chief 7idansuu looked at him.

"You told me, and your uncle told you, that the spirit, the essence, must be caught, and the identifying symbol emphasized, that the space must be beautifully filled. But there's something else, Uncle, something you didn't tell me. Something I found out for myself." He turned a glistening black sculpture in his hands. "I found out that change is a challenge. An exciting challenge!"

A small glow leapt up in his uncle's sad eyes.

"Change frees a man, Uncle."

"Da·axiigang." The chief said the name tenderly. Then tears overcame the last of the old-style Haida chiefs.

CHANGE IS A CHALLENGE," 7idansuu told himself fiercely. "Change frees a man."

This change was a bitter, personal defeat for one of the proudest and wealthiest families in Haida Gwaii. But they took it like the aristocrats they were. They effected the change with style. A family of artists, they decorated even their humiliation. A public people, they dressed up their defeat and made it a dignified occasion.

They were baptized that very year of 1884.

Mr. Collison's successor, the Reverend Mr. Harrison of the Massett Mission, was delighted. He was a trifle confused, though, by the chief's insistence that he should have gone to

England and married the queen's daughter. He couldn't quite see the relevance of the comment.

"You mightn't have married the queen's daughter even if you had gone to England," he consoled 7idansuu. "English princesses marry kings, you know."

"Am I not a king here?" 7idansuu demanded to know.

"You are indeed," the missionary assured him. "And we'll give you a king's name."

Albert Edward Edenshaw, he wrote into the records. Sun-Lak-Kwee-Kun became Amy Edenshaw. Their son became Henry Edenshaw.

"But my son is a Raven like his mother," Albert Edward Edenshaw protested. "They can't wear the Eagle name 7idansuu."

"Tut, tut." Mr. Harrison dismissed any such nonsense about names. "Tut, tut." There was only one proper way to name women and children, after the father's family name. He wrote in the three names with a firm hand.

Next, Mr. Harrison considered a suitable name for Da·axiigang. "The crown prince, isn't he?" he remarked affably. A pretender unlikely to do much ruling, he thought to himself, like Bonnie Prince Charlie of Scotland. Charles Edenshaw, he named Da·axiigang.

Da·axiigang's chieftainess chose her own name. She considered many queens' names before settling on Isabella.

When Mr. Harrison christened her Isabella Edenshaw and addressed her as "Mrs. Edenshaw," she didn't bother to protest that she wasn't entitled to wear the Eagle name either. The less you explained to white men, the better you got along with them. Every native person knew that. White men lived within a precise wall. Everything contained by that wall was "proper"; everything outside that wall was "heathen practice" and, of course, wicked.

"You're lucky you got off with nothing worse than a wrong

name," 7idansuu joked to her when they reached home. "Remember what happened at Fort Simpson!"

At Fort Simpson, over the indignant howls of the whole village, a missionary had insisted on marrying a young couple. He was resolutely making a stand against "the heathen practice of buying brides," so nothing could budge him. He married the young couple with righteous enthusiasm. And he never did understand that by marrying an Eagle boy to an Eagle girl, he deeply shamed two fine Tsimshian families and scandalized the whole coast.

Chief 7idansuu formally presented the name of 7idansuu to each of his close relatives. "Now it's yours to wear," he said, making them more comfortable in their new names.

Da·axiigang's heir already had an Iron name, Charles Gladstone, like his white father.

"How does the queen dress?" Isabella asked Mrs. Harrison. "How does she dress her children?"

Mrs. Harrison showed her pictures of the British royal family; and Isabella discussed the fashions with Amy.

"We dress like that from now on," the two chieftainesses informed their family, "except at home and at camp, and perhaps in the canoes," they conceded.

Officially, the Edenshaws now had no slaves to serve them. But their old servants stayed on like relatives; they were happy to paddle the state canoe to Victoria the following summer to buy clothing appropriate to the family's new names and new status as Christians.

Albert Edward Edenshaw's new clothing included one formal outfit with silk top hat for dress occasions. He carved a gold-headed cane to go with it.

The Haida ladies brightened their new rustling black silks with gold Killer Whale earrings and bracelets. Neither could resist letting her luxuriant hair fall down to her bustle at the back, though it was pulled back neatly from a center parting.

Charles Edenshaw contented himself with quiet suits; he fashioned his favorite Frog crest into a gold tiepin.

Without their identifying crests, they would have felt like social outcasts.

"And now," Albert Edward Edenshaw told his villagers, "so that our young people may learn to read and to play in a brass band, we'll build a house at Massett. We'll live there in the winter and come back here each spring. But," he added firmly, "we'll build our Massett house in the old style."

On the mainland, as the young Haida were always impatiently pointing out to their elders, the Tsimshian were tearing down their old-fashioned houses to build lumber houses with windows.

"I refuse to live in an ugly house," the chief stated flatly. "And," he went on, eyeing the young people almost defiantly, "we'll name it Potlatch House."

Old style or new style, the young people were thrilled at the prospect of moving to Massett. They were convinced that only speedy acquisition of the white man's ways would bring back to the Haida their old position as lords of the coast. They were eager "to get out of the blanket."

Older people were as willing to move. The Haida race was still clearly dying out; though now it was consumption, not smallpox, that was ravaging the villages. They were haunted by Kwanduhadgaa's vision. They were deeply convinced that only Massett and Skidegate would indeed survive God's wrath.

They moved to Massett, and the young people went eagerly to church and to mission school. They adopted new ways with enthusiasm. "And when are you going to get out of the blanket?" they demanded, not altogether jokingly, of their parents and grandparents. "The chief dresses like a white man."

"Not always," the parents retorted.

Children actually began to shrink away in embarrassment from old Haida myths except when they found themselves caught in the spell of Chief 7idansuu's Raven story. They deliberately stifled the thought that it truly was easier to believe tales filled with birds and sea monsters and killer whales and salmon and tree spirits and primeval clamshells than it was to believe tales about a camel in a desert, or about chariots and Romans and palm leaves and an ass.

Adam and Eve were the first people on earth, they told themselves, and not the tiny creatures Raven released from a clamshell on Rose Spit.

People survived the Flood in an ark full of elephants and giraffes, they reminded one another; they didn't really climb Ƙingii's totem pole or escape in a canoe.

A dove brought an olive branch to signal the end of the Flood; eagles didn't really shake down their feathers to still the rising waters.

But it was awfully hard to stop believing one thing and start believing something else. Still, the white man was right, everyone knew that.

Young people even began to scorn the old Haida decoration, except, of course, when visiting white chiefs showed obvious admiration for Chief Da·aẋiigang's (Charles Edenshaw's) work. Few youths betrayed any ambition to carve.

This change in attitude among the young was accelerated by the arrival of a new Hudson's Bay trader with twelve children and stepchildren. The Alexanders (with a few O'Neills) came to Massett on the steamer *Sardonyx* in May 1890.

"They can read fast," Haida children reported wistfully to their relatives. "They can write better than we can." They hated to be inferior to anybody in anything. One thing they had not been able to put behind them was the Haida compulsion to excel. Yet envy and admiration were not altogether on one side.

"Haida girls have such beautiful hair!" ten-year-old Martha O'Neill told her mother, Mrs. Alexander.

Martha O'Neill had been enchanted with the totem pole villages all the way up the coast. At Fort Simpson, where she counted thirteen warships and hundreds of native people camped along the shore, she had written in her diary: "It's a lovely sight on a beautiful night when their tents and campfires line the beach and you can hear the laughter of the small papooses playing tag around the beached canoes." Massett, with its wealth of totem poles and ornamented houses, looked even lovelier to her. "And Haida girls have such beautiful hair!" she told her diary.

Her brothers' envy and admiration were stirred by the Haida boys' skill in dropping a blue grouse with one swift stone, aimed at the neck.

Their mother was as wistful over the sea otter cloaks the chieftainesses wore. "Sea otter fur is the single most beautiful thing I've ever seen in my life," she declared, running her fingers through long, silky, black fur brightened by occasional silver hairs. The pelts had been brought in to the trading post and were being readied for shipment to London. "Look," she coaxed her husband, "I sold my own saddle horse and kept my own money for something special. And this is what I want, a sea otter cloak. Well, a sea otter cape maybe," she said, more realistically.

"And this is what you can't have," Mr. Alexander informed her. "The charter gave all the fur in Canada to the Company. It's going to the Company. All nine pelts!" Nine sea otter skins were that whole year's take from the Queen Charlotte Islands.

"Company men!" his wife snorted. And she went on envying the Haida chieftainesses.

That was a sad time for several Haida chieftainesses. Gu·uu had developed the only too prevalent symptoms of consumption and died the previous September; his mother had died shortly before him.

7idansuu was shaken by his loss. But the rhythm of the seasons must go on, he knew. That was the law of life. So, after the Christian burial of Gu·uu, he and a group of families harvested the crab apples near Rose Spit. And they were camped on the east shore, a little south of the spit, when they saw the *Sardonyx* pass on her last trip of the season.

Suddenly, an extraordinary thing happened. The sea heaved without warning. The *Sardonyx* was lifted up and hurled onto a reef. Giant waves raced shoreward.

Instantly the chief and his men launched canoes into the dangerous seas. They managed to rescue everybody.

"Must have been an undersea earthquake," said Captain Smith of the *Sardonyx*. Gratefully he watched the Haida tend half-drowned men and set broken bones with the skills they had developed through centuries of seafaring isolation. He saw them summon help by canoe.

When help arrived and he was leaving his rescuers, Captain Smith began a formal speech of thanks to Chief 7idansuu. Then he stopped. He looked straight at the figure before him, majestic in sea otter cloak and crest-painted canoe hat. In an instinctive gesture of honor and respect, he laid his gun at the chief's feet. And every Haida straightened his shoulders and lifted a proud head.

Albert Edward Edenshaw won a different tribute from Mrs. Alexander at Massett. "I'm convinced he's a white man," she said to her family. "I'm sure he was stolen away by the Indians when he was a baby."

She was even more convinced of this when he paid a call

on the family on New Year's Day. He arrived wearing formal attire and his silk top hat, and carrying his gold-headed cane. He chatted amiably, nibbled Christmas cake, sipped Hudson's Bay rum. Then he invited the Alexanders (and the O'Neills) to his house for the evening.

When they arrived at Potlatch House at eight o'clock, they found a huge fire blazing on a hearth that was glisteningly white with broken clamshells. Dancers waited on both sides of the fire, their costumes and fantastic dance masks colorful in the firelight. Chiefs and subchiefs waited in patterned Chilkat blankets and crowns filled with ceremonial swan's-down. Drums were beating.

The excited Alexanders (and the excited O'Neills) were seated on cedar mats on an upper tier of the old-style feasthouse, high above the dancers. They saw people begin swaying and chanting. And, to a burst of acclaim, the head chief of the Sdast'a·aas Eagles appeared from behind a screen. He, too, wore his deeply fringed Chilkat blanket; and as he slowly circled the lodge, shaking his bird rattle, he wafted swan's-down from his crown of sea lion bristles. He took his place on the beautifully carved seat at the rear of the house. Above him and behind him, the great Eagle spread his wings.

"I do believe he is an Indian after all," Mrs. Alexander whispered.

The dancers began to move gracefully. And as they moved, eagle-down and swan's-down swirled everywhere, caught in drafts from the great fire.

"Oh, Mama! Mama!" Martha O'Neill cried. "It's like snowflakes dancing. Oh, Mama! It's so lovely!"

Albert Edward Edenshaw lived for only three more New Year's Day dances in Potlatch House. And when this last of the old-style Haida chiefs died, in 1894, there was no totem pole raised in his honor on the shores of Haida Gwaii. There was a gray tombstone, starkly engraved by white men. There was a memorial stone in the village, citing only his service to the white men of the *Susan Sturgis*. There were several eulogies in the newspapers. The one written by Mr. Harrison ended with this paragraph:

> Farewell, It-in-sa, the manly brave and the truest chief that ever existed among the Haidas, and the truest friend of the white man that we white men could possibly come into contact with. *Requiescat in Pace!*

Fewer than six hundred natives survived him in Haida Gwaii; and there was much sickness among the six hundred. The race was dying out. The social order was dying out even faster.

Charles Edenshaw, Da·axiigang, did what he could to let both die with dignity. He assumed the head chieftainship of the Sdast'a·aas Eagles with quiet ceremony. He continued to give feasts at intervals, and to distribute gifts to the people.

But his whole being was caught up in a strange compulsion. His race was dying out; and he could not stop the dying. His social order was dying out; and he could only see that it died with the dignity of the Haida. But one thing was too strong to die, Haida art! Its strength pulsed through frail Da·axiigang.

It was as though the unique style of decoration, developed through thousands of years of life in an environment that was fabulously rich and yet chill and challenging, was too strong to die with the people and the social order that had nurtured it. Now, threatened with extinction, it worked like a compulsion through Da·axiigang, like a disembodied spirit using the fingers of Charles Edenshaw. It would live on! This man was a link between its past and its future.

Apart from this distinctively Haida compulsion to excel in

art, the Edenshaws resembled the admired British royal family more than they ever knew. Just as the ancient Haida use of ermine skins to denote the exact status of the wearer had amazingly paralleled the British use of ermine at the Court of St. James, so now the Haida pattern of influence again paralleled that of the British royal family, though the noble House of Windsor might have been astounded to hear this stated.

Deprived by law of their right to rule, they set themselves the high duty of being an example and an inspiration to their people. They lived as an affectionately united family; yet various members used their immense prestige and influence in differing ways. Together, they cherished and preserved tradition while still making a stand for progress.

Sun-Lak-Kwee-Kun, now a handsome woman in her forties, maintained Potlatch House with old-style pride in its beauty. Wood was rubbed until it shone. Every week the pebbles and clamshells were replaced to keep the hearth gleaming white in the firelight. And when not-too-industrious young helpers ventured to ask her why, she did not confuse their Christian minds by telling them it was to please and honor the household spirits. She simply said, "It's unlucky to be dirty." And nobody dared to be dirty.

In the old way of Haida chieftainesses, she went camping with the group on fishing and berrying expeditions. She even went to the mainland fish canneries with them. Yet she continued to win from them an almost breathless respect. The most emancipated child was struck dumb with awe when Her Serene Highness approached. She was the traditional, reverenced Chief Mother of the matrilineal Haida!

Isabella and Charles Edenshaw's children dearly loved to go camping with "High Grandmother." They begged to travel in her big canoe, and to stay with her in Potlatch House. They themselves now lived in a house with doors and windows and an iron stove and a lighted back room for their father's work. They traveled the coast in a yacht with sails and an engine.

It was the lack of slaves that drove Charles Edenshaw to an Iron boat; it was Haida family feeling that made him ask one of his Raven fathers from Skidegate to captain it.

It was progress that made him provide himself with an efficient workshop; it was his Haida heart that filled the workshop, at times, with gifted young relatives.

His heir, Charlie Gladstone, was gifted but disinterested. A lively boy who was eager to "get out of the blanket," Charlie developed a scorn for Yaahl the Raven and Tsing the Beaver and the other mythological characters his uncle depicted. He began to see the old social order, too, as a lot of nonsense. As his own mother pointed out, on visits from Victoria, why should he mortgage his future to keep up old customs? The old days were dead. He renounced his claim to the chieftainship, left Massett, married, and settled down in Skidegate as a commercial fisherman.

The chief sighed at this loss of his heir; Charlie had been a favorite with the whole family. But it was the work that really mattered. And he still had his only son, Ginaawaan, Robert.

"Ginaawaan's the most gifted of them all," Charles Edenshaw told his wife. "He'll carry on my work when I go."

Even with this assurance, he worked like a driven man to record in silver and gold, in wood and slate, and in salmon-egg paint and pencil, the art and mythology of the Haida.

Isabella watched both husband and son with pride. She supported her husband's roles as Haida chief, Christian leader, commercial artist, and family man with the happy affection of a wife and mother, and also with the drive of a chieftainess. She helped Sun-Lak-Kwee-Kun keep up the old ways; she continued to weave spruce-root hats; she never failed to lay spruce needles along her babies' noses to make them grow prettier.

Yet she was ruthlessly modern. She was determined to dress her children the way the queen dressed her children.

"I'm sure the queen has a sewing machine," she said one day to her husband.

"You'll have one too," he promised, "as soon as we can afford it."

The Potlatch Law had stopped the returning tide of wealth that should have been flowing in to the present Chief 7idansuu, since his predecessor had given ten lavish potlatches. Charles Edenshaw had only what he could earn. Slate poles sold for fifty cents an inch; two weeks' work might bring in six dollars. And much of his earnings as a commercial artist went to maintain his responsibilities as a Haida chief.

Still, eked out by the bounty of Haida waters, his earnings kept his family and also supported some dignity in the social order. The work itself kept Haida art alive in spite of local indifference to it. The Killer Whale and the Raven and Tsing were old-fashioned and heathen, people said; you had to turn your back on them, now. You had to get out of the blanket!

There was no scorn for the Killer Whale and the Raven and Tsing in scholarly and artistic circles in faraway Washington, New York, London, Berlin.

Day after day after day he worked: carving slate, hammering gold, and engraving silver. He adapted the ancient arrangements of flattened ovals into stunning new patterns; he squeezed the old, abstracted elements of the mythological characters into new shapes, new designs, new beauty. And always, he showed each finished piece to his family with pride.

"It's beautiful!" they would assure him, excitedly turning a Killer Whale bracelet to catch the light.

"It's wonderful!" they'd say, standing in awe before the dramatic elegance of a Salmon Prince argillite plate.

"It is nice," he would agree. And to his son he would add,

"It's so good to be clever, Ginaawaan! And we could be poor if it weren't for this work."

"Instead, we're rich," Isabella sometimes commented, almost sharply. "Rich enough to buy a sewing machine?"

"We'll get you a sewing machine, dear," her husband continued to promise.

Each time he showed a piece of work to his family, he told them the story it illustrated.

"But the story's not really true," his children reminded one another, later.

Working for the big American museums, he made argillite replicas of storage boxes; and the beauty of the traditional designs, enhanced by the luster of polished slate, thrilled him a thousand times. The designs were so perfect. So utterly refined and flawless! Always, the central figure caught your eye; beautifully controlled lines led your eye to a corner, and then around and around. There was no end to the pattern of flattened ovals. There was no escape from the box design.

When the American Museum of Natural History ordered a gigantic war canoe, Edenshaw was commissioned to decorate it. Behind a sculptured Wolf figurehead, he designed a Raven clan's Killer Whale, compressing the huge head into the tapering confines of the thrusting prow. He added a human tongue to show that this was no mere killer whale; this was Killer Whale, supernatural sea beast! He pressed back the towering, slicing, dorsal fin to be contained by the rim of the ship. The Killer Whale felt the confinement of the cedar. If he could burst those bonds, it seemed to say, if he could surge forward, and through, into the sea! But there was no escape. On the stern, Edenshaw painted an Eagle, giving him a human eye to indicate his mythological dual nature.

"It's magnificent! Superb!" his family told him when the canoe was finished.

"It is nice when it falls together and fits," he confessed to them. Secretly he delighted in the pride and joy he saw reflected in his son's eyes. Ginaawaan would finish the work his father had only started.

Ginaawaan was eighteen in 1896, the year they finally decided they would buy the sewing machine for Isabella. This time, when they sailed south to Victoria to sell slate and silver pieces, they would let her feel like a queen, at last!

To help afford the thing his mother craved, Ginaawaan left the yacht at Rivers Inlet to visit High Grandmother and work with other native people at a fish cannery. He arranged to catch the *Princess Louise,* a coastal steamer, on her run north, later. He would meet his family at Fort Simpson, where they also went annually to sell argillite and silver. Then the whole family would go back to Massett together, bearing the sewing machine home in triumph.

The family went to Victoria, bought the yearned-for machine, and then sailed north to Fort Simpson. They gathered joyously on the wharf when the *Princess Louise* steamed in.

Ginaawaan did not come down the gangplank with the other passengers.

The family waited patiently, watching the ship's unloading. They saw a coffin lowered. Still, Ginaawaan did not get off the steamer.

Then someone broke the news to the family. Ginaawaan had been drowned at Rivers Inlet. Their beloved boy was in the coffin.

Friends and relatives clustered about the bereaved family, first at Fort Simpson, then at Massett. But Charles Edenshaw seemed beyond comfort.

"What shall I do?" he asked over and over and over. It was as though he grieved for two: himself and Haida art. "I never knew a man could suffer so much," he muttered. He was so distracted with grief that once he turned on Isabella. "If you hadn't insisted on having a sewing machine," he said, "you might have had your son." Then he stayed silent in his workshop. When he touched his tools, it was only to lament about them. "They would have been so useful to him!" he kept saying.

He had lost his heir, and now his son.

Then he plunged into work. More than ever before, he worked like a driven man. Now there would be no one who could truly design when he died. There were only men who would copy in their spare time, never quite understanding the work they did. He worked endlessly, tirelessly; and his art reached a new perfection.

The American Museum of Natural History sent the Jesup Expedition to the northwest coast at the beginning of the twentieth century. Now, when it was too late, Dr. Swanton and his fellow-scientists arrived on the Queen Charlotte Islands to record Haida culture. They enlisted Charles Edenshaw's help.

He made scores of wood and slate models for them, including a model of Myth House. He identified stylized characters for them. He sketched tattoo patterns, and he drew original illustrations of Haida customs. He gave them a wealth of information. But there was too much to tell, too much to show the white man.

He did not, perhaps could not, convey to them the principles of the design style he worked in. Possibly he believed that only by working in it could a man learn its secrets and its potential.

After the scientists left, he continued to work without respite. But he could never finish, there was no end to the things he wanted, and needed, to do.

In 1910, his health gave way at last beneath his surging spirit. Consumption began to wrack his body. "If only I knew how to give my hands to your sons," he kept saying to his daughters. It was the work that mattered, not himself.

It had never occurred to him that his daughters might have learned to carve and paint. Haida women did not do that.

In 1920, he died in obscurity on the native reserve at Massett.

He was survived by two villages: Massett and Skidegate.

More than a quarter of a century later, Charlie Gladstone's grandson began to experience a strange compulsion to carve, to engrave silver, to make bracelets and earrings like those treasured as heirlooms by relatives at Skidegate and Massett.

Bill Reid was twenty-eight, and had had no previous desire to be any kind of artist or craftsman. An educated city man, he had chosen to be a radio broadcaster. In fact, he was working in the Toronto studios of the Canadian Broadcasting Corporation when he felt the irresistible urge.

He enrolled in an engraving course in his spare time; he joined jewelry-making classes. And he found himself oddly critical of the models he studied; he knew they were not good, but he did not know how he knew it. The men who are jewelers can't design, he observed to himself; and the men who are designers have no technique as jewelers.

He looked again at family heirlooms, with new appreciation. "Great-Uncle Charlie Edenshaw must have been the only jeweler in the world whose work was truly art," he commented to the family.

He felt compelled to find Great-Uncle Charlie Edenshaw's work in museums. They had something special, he knew—a tenseness, an excitement, a beauty that thrilled him. Lines were so tense, clean, and elegant. And everywhere was the "ovoid," the flattened oval. It was here an eye, there a joint or the leading edge of a bird's wing or the fin of a killer whale. Edenshaw's art seemed to him to be like variations on a single note in music.

He knew he had to do work like that. He did not know why he had to do it. He just had to.

Yet how could he learn the principles of Haida design? Even Boas's book, and Swanton's, were unable to tell him. And old Skidegate relatives who were still chipping slate worked, he saw, as straight copyists. Often they copied from pictures of slate poles they found in museum books.

He began to study totem poles: the few old ones still standing, the new ones men were chipping in Victoria, Port Simpson (Fort Simpson). Some were good; some were bad. A good totem pole was truly terrifying. It seemed to be a concentration of enormous tensions, as if something were trying to break out, as if a conflict were trying to resolve itself. It seemed to be wound up tight, like a spring. If the characters could just break out of a good pole, he felt, what might they not do? And a poor pole? If the characters in an inferior totem pole lost the support of the cedar, he felt, they would flop into a blob on the ground.

What was the secret?

He began working to find out.

He began to work like a driven man.

He certainly did not want to be a totem pole chipper. Yet he found himself abandoning the security of a CBC job for the hazards of Haida art. He found himself agreeing to build a "Haida village" for the University of British Columbia. And, like the ghost of Great-Uncle Charlie Edenshaw that seemed to hover near him, he found joy in the work. Carving was a wonderful release from his own tensions, he discovered. When it worked out well, he experienced a surge of joy.

"There were ghosts there the whole time I worked," he confides now. As he chipped at red cedars, he felt first one presence. "Oh, I know it was the loneliness and the gray light and the hypnotic rhythm of the chipping," he explains, "but Great-Uncle

Charlie was there with me every minute." He kept sensing what Charles Edenshaw wanted him to do. He felt constant guidance in his work. "I had to do it his way," he says. "Great-Uncle Charlie was there. And the old ladies were with him."

The "old ladies" were the ghosts of Haida chieftainesses; they joined the ghost of Charles Edenshaw around the totem poles that were being carved at the university in Vancouver.

"They watched every move I made," he insists. "I felt their criticism. I had to do it their way."

The ghosts stayed with him until he had built the "Haida village." They lingered on even when the opening ceremonies had been scheduled and the platform guests invited.

Why did they linger?

"They wanted me to potlatch it," he says, with a strange acceptance of the Haida ghosts and their wishes. "I had to potlatch it. I had to! The old ladies made me do it."

He did potlatch it, though in secret. Without telling the university committee why, he made a silver crest medallion, at his own expense, for each of the "witnesses" on the platform; he set the medallions into cedar left over from the totem poles. He asked an understanding fellow Haida, Dr. Peter Kelly, to serve as his "distributor" at the "potlatch."

After the potlatch, the chieftainesses left him. But Charles Edenshaw did not leave him. The ghost of the greatest of all Haida artists simply moved into his great-grandnephew's workshop.

"Great-Uncle Charlie is my superego," the modern Haida artist says, being a sophisticated man. And he works away in his haunted workshop year after year, carving argillite into exciting designs and polishing it until it glistens like a raven's wing; engraving the Eagle and the Killer Whale and the Salmon Prince on gold and silver. His slate sculptures are treasured by collectors; his Haida jewelry is worn by smart women in Vancouver, London, Paris, Moscow.

Each piece is stamped "HAIDA ART" in clear print. In smaller letters, it is signed "Reid." It is the "Haida Art" that is important to the man haunted by Charles Edenshaw's ghost.

"Haida society was expendable," he says. "What has emerged as worthwhile is the art. Charles Edenshaw's work was the distillation of thousands of years of evolution in one decorative style. And some genius must discover it, as Picasso discovered African art, and evolve a great new art form. But, until that genius comes along . . ."

Until that genius comes along, perhaps the last great Chief 7idansuu will not be free to go off to the Land of Souls. Perhaps Haida art is holding him as the link between a great past and a great future.

"Critics don't quite believe Haida art," its modern disciple says. "It's so refined and highly evolved that they can't believe it emerged from an aboriginal culture."

After all, as the old fur traders told their shipmates, these were only savages; they hadn't fine feelings like civilized human beings.

Maybe a more enlightened generation will know better.

G L O S S A R Y

Here is a list of Haida names and words, and their more familiar renderings in historical and ethnographic records.

Da·axiigang	Tahayghen
Gannyaa	Gunya
Ginaawaan	Gyinawen
Gu·uu	Gao
Gwaii gang·hling	Gwai-gwun-thlin
Haida Gwaii	Queen Charlotte Islands
Haiias	Haias
7idansuu	Edenshaw
7wii·aa	Weah

Ḵingii	Qingk
Ḵung	Ḵung
Kwanduhadgaa	Condohahtgha
K'yuusdaa	Kiusta
Lagaahl	Legaic
Massett	Masset
Niikun	Ne-Kwun
Saang gaahl	Shongalth
Sdast'a·aas	Stastas
Sdiihldaa	Steilta
Siigee	Seegay
Skawal	Skoual
Skulkin nagaas	Skulkinanse
Sudaahl	Sudal
Taawhlgee	Tahlee
Tlaas kwun	Klas-kwun
Waaniiks	Wineeks
Wiiba	Wiba
Yaahl	Yelth
Yaakun	Ya-kan
Yaan	Yan
Yatz	Yatza